Ingleborough

Dales books
by W R Mitchell

A DALESMAN'S DIARY
HIGH DALE COUNTRY
DRYSTONE WALLS OF THE YORKSHIRE DALES
THE CHANGING DALES
YORKSHIRE DALESFOLK
DALESFOLK TALKING
WILD PENNINES
PENNINE BIRDS
A YEAR WITH THE CURLEWS
THREE PEAKS AND MALHAMDALE
A WALK ACROSS THE YORKSHIRE DALES
YORKSHIRE DALES A TO Z

INGLEBOROUGH
The Big Blue Hill

by W R Mitchell

Ingleborough from Thornton-in-Lonsdale.

CASTLEBERG
1994

To a bare blue hill
Wings an old thought
    roaming,
At a random touch
Of memory homing.

Laurence Binyon, about Ingleborough.

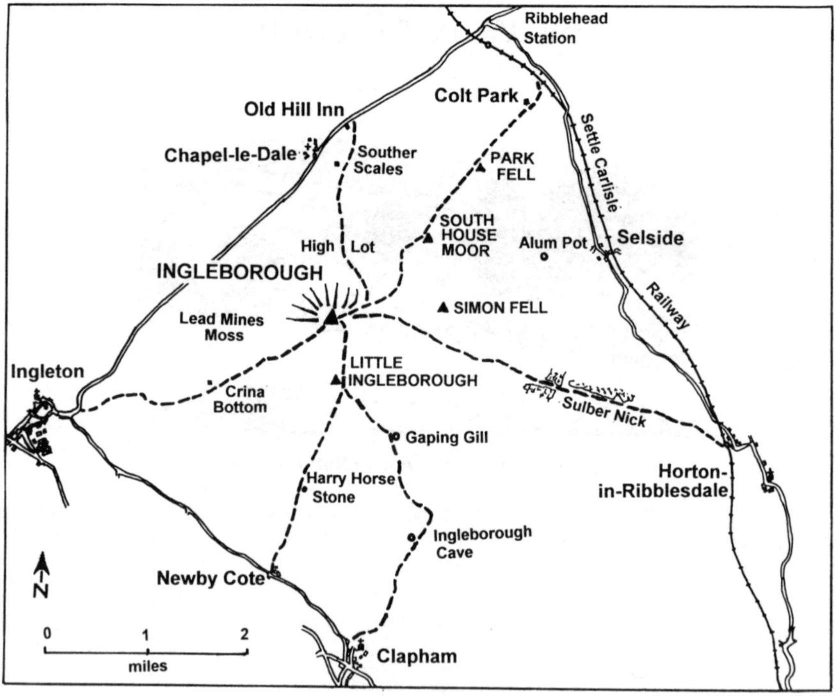

Published by Castleberg, 18 Yealand Avenue, Giggleswick,
Settle, North Yorkshire, BD24 0AY

Typeset in Clearface and printed by Lamberts Printers,
Station Road, Settle, North Yorkshire, BD24 9AA

ISBN: 1 871064 87 2

Contents

Ingleborough may be said to take precedence of all the Yorkshire mountains; it stands prominent before the rest, and forms on its summit a spacious plain (said to be a mile in circumference), whereon might almost stand the adult population of the county.

Thomas Wilkinson, Tours to the British Mountains, 1824.

Ingleborough, Whernside and Penyghent
Are the highest hills twixt Tweed and Trent.

Old Couplet.

Like most Yorkshiremen, I was taught in my boyhood to regard Ingleborough as a sort of Everest...

Alfred J Brown, Moorland Tramping in West Yorkshire, 1931.

Ingleborough...is probably the most ascended mountain in the country outside Lakeland.

Alfred Wainwright.

The great hill has many moods. Ramblers who have made the ascent in mist find a world of sunshine on its crest...Visitors who have started the climb under the bluest of blue skies have returned drenched.

Albert Mitchell, Under Ingleborough.

Ingleborough, the 'king-hill' of the Park...a piece of country known, if only cartographically, to practically every schoolchild who has taken 'O' level geography.

Guide to the Yorkshire Dales National Park, 1971.

Ingleborough has an English name. It is 'Ingeld's fortress', a reference to the ancient hillfort, while Ingeld probably had an estate here, for Ingleton nearby is 'Ingeld's farm'.

Richard Muir, 1991.

First Impressions

AN orange-painted *Pennine* bus, with Lile Jackie at the wheel, descended Cave Ha', just north of Settle, in north-west Yorkshire. Cool air, whistling through its radiator, cooled off the engine after the long drag up Buckhaw Brow, against a backdrop of Giggleswick Scars.

Jackie, a thin-faced man with Brylcreamed black hair, had his breakfast at this stage of the journey. He kept the bus on the road by grasping the steering wheel with his right hand while his left hand groped for, located and delivered to his mouth the sandwiches in what he called his bait-bag.

On that journey almost fifty years ago, the road had not altered much since the turnpike days of the eighteenth century. The *Pennine* bus, one of a valiant little fleet, had been given its distinctive colour because on a visit to Leylands to buy their first vehicle in the 1920s, the Simpson brothers had taken a fancy to the orange-sided bus being used by the works' football team.

I was on my way to spend a week-end with the Scotts of Clapham prior to joining Harry J Scott on his relatively new Yorkshire magazine, *The Yorkshire Dalesman.* Those were the days when people queued for buses. Passengers were crowded to a degree which sardines would find insufferable.

The bus I was using had twenty passengers—twenty-one, if you count the goat. I recall that, at the approach to Settle, the landscape brightened with the appearance of the limestone. Beyond the shallow Ribble Valley and Giggleswick's domed chapel, perched on a gritstone knoll, the skyline was crowned by a flat-topped hill, part of a group of hills which sprawled languidly, giving the impression of a lion at rest. Distance and cloud shadow gave the hill a blue tinge.

At Buckhaw Brow, I heard the fanciful tale of horses which bucked because they detected the lingering odour of ancient beasts whose remains were found in local caves. It was a morning of such clarity that, from Cave Ha', I had a momentary glimpse of the Cumbrian fells, spread across the far northern skyline. They resembled molars on a gum of green.

When, near Rawlinshaw, the big blue hill came back into view, now rising above pearl-white limestone, the old farmer sitting beside me said: 'That's Ingleborough. . . It's a big rough hill. And wild! The wind's often strong enough to blow a sheep ower. I wouldn't be capped [surprised] to see snow up there on Midsummer's Day.'

Ingleborough—one of the big Pennine flat-tops—almost shouted to be noticed. 'Aye,' said the farmer. 'I used to tend sheep on yon 'ill. Once I went up to gather some. Mist came down. I were lost. At t'finish, I got back to t'farm by following t'sheep.' He uttered a wheezy laugh.

During the week-end, I saw Ingleborough from Newby Moor and, again, it was the blueness which impressed. I was introduced to Matthew Farrer, the squire, one of a family who became important local landowners in the eighteenth century. I chatted with Arnold Brown—Cave Guide Brown—who conducted visitors through Ingleborough Cave by candlelight.

Travelling by bus to Ingleton, I had further tantalising glimpses of t'gurt hill, with its stepped topography, caused by horizontal layers of limestones, shales and grits. The *Pennine* had conductors then. As the bus neared its destination, this worthy announced, in a dramatic voice and with a wry smile, 'Ingleton—land of Waterfalls and Caves'.

I had intended to sub-title this book 'fire mountain', but that sounds too melodramatic, giving an erroneous impression that Ingleborough, the most popular hill in Yorkshire, is a spent volcano instead of just an accumulation of sediments in sea and delta. The writers who played with fire had been mis-led by 'ingle', their thoughts springing to Ingleborough's status as a beacon hill.

So, in a literary sense, I switched from Red to Blue. It is not always blue, of course. Yet it was the blue tinge which first impressed me. And that blueness inspired Laurence Binyon, son of the first vicar of Burton-in-Lonsdale, to write his first poem.

Binyon would grow up to become an academic and poet, renowned as the author of 'Words to the Fallen', which we recite each Remembrance Day. Yet he never forgot his childhood view of Ingleton from the Burton vicarage and in boyhood he wrote:

To a bare blue hill
Wings an old thought roaming,
At a random touch
Of memory homing.

The first of England
These eyes to fill
Was the lifted head
Of that proud hill . . .

I have seen that 'lifted head' from Pendle, from Great Shunner Fell, from beside the Big Stone of Fourstone above Bentham, from several Lakeland peaks and from Wet Sahara, as someone called the sands of Morecambe Bay, exposed at low tide. When following the line of the former coach route from Hest Bank to Kents Bank, in the company of Cedric Robinson, the Sands Guide, I discovered that Ingleborough was keeping its eye on me.

My favourite view is from Twistleton Scars, just across the deep trough of Chapel-le-Dale. On a bright January day, when the few hardy sheep are rummaging for grass among the clints [blocks of limestone] and the only sound is the honking of a peevish crow, I stare entranced at the hill which the eighteenth-century poet Gray called 'this huge creature of god'.

In January, the sun appears, spins a few times—and is gone. To an observer on Twistleton Scars, the laggard sun bursts into view between Ingleborough Hill and Simon Fell. By the time I have traversed the Scars, under the solemn gaze of Dales-bred sheep, now chewing the cud, it is time for a drink and snack. When I begin the return journey, the sun is well on its way to its destination, beyond the silver sheen of Morecambe Bay.

Sunlight picks out the terraces between the three main tiers of limestone which form the plinth on which Ingleborough proper is standing. What were dark shadows are now expanses of blues and greys, edged by white, the cores of old snowdrifts.

At the time of the last glaciation, Ingleborough was a nunatak—an island of rock rising above the ice, glistening white but with powder-blue shadows. In winter, the hill seems devoid of life, even of sheep, which are brought down to graze the better pastures. Yet the fat buds of alpine flowers will soon be evident on the high cliffs and the dragonfly nymph lives beneath the ice on peaty pools.

Ingleborough was revered by Reginald Farrer (1880-1920), writer and plant-collector, who was reared at Ingleborough Hall, Clapham, at the southern rim of the hill. An emotional man, who once prostrated himself before a plant he found appealing, Farrer had his sympathies and sense of colour aroused to fever pitch when he saw Ingleborough, the 'great mountain', which 'lies lazily against heavy cloud masses in the west, the long, sleepy lines of its eastern slope looming dark, in blue and violet, against the gloom behind...'

Farrer's spirit still broods over Ingleborough. It was his vivid prose which prompted me to make the first of many expeditions

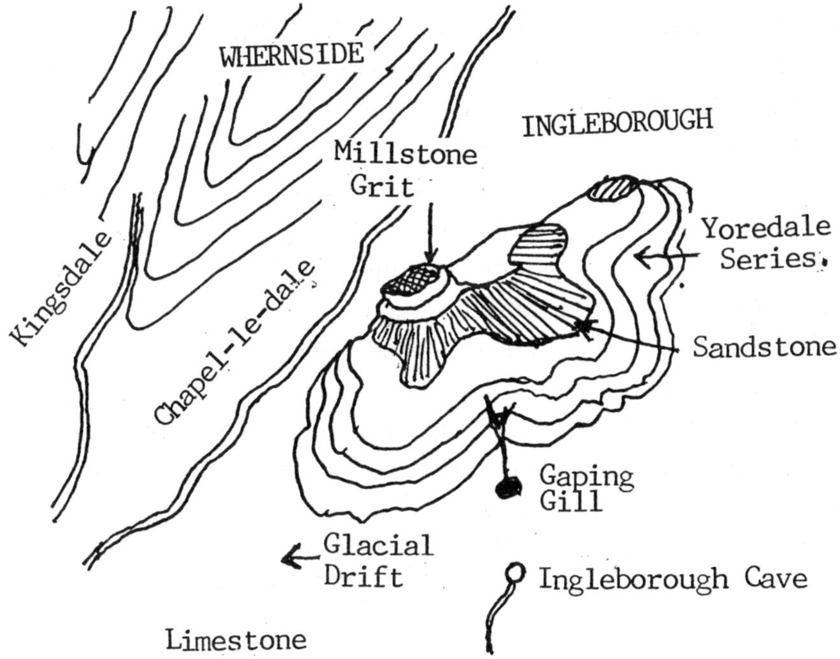

to the summit of the hill. Ingleborough has more to attract a visitor than its two famous neighbours—Whernside and Penyghent—because the approaches are over more interesting and varied ground.

On my first trip to Ingleborough summit, I took the scenic route, through the woods, beside the lake, up the dry valley, by Ingleborough Cave and Trow Gill to the funnel-shaped hole of Gaping Gill (the old north-country gill, not the Wordsworthian ghyll). It was springtime and the snow had melted. I was told about the potholer who some years before inadvertently walked over the main shaft (340 ft deep) on a cornice of snow.

One of the few unsolved mysteries of Ingleborough dates back to August, 1947, when two potholers found a man's skeleton in Trow Gill. His clothing had rotted but the contents of his pockets, including pen, watch, razor, a bottle and unbroken ampoule, the last two containing cyanide, remained intact. Had he been a German spy? A week later, more human bones were found in the main chamber of G.G., less than half a mile away.

The story was to gather an aura from imaginative story-telling.

From Gaping Gill, I undertook the short drag to Little Ingleborough, thence to what the Ordnance Survey still calls Ingleborough Hill, though by elevation it qualifies as a mountain. Far from diminishing Ingleborough's status, the term 'hill' enhances it, as a plain 'Mister' distinguishes a consultant in the world of medicine.

On that first climb, I had the summit of Ingleborough to myself. A contemporary guide book described the track from Gaping Gill as 'almost non-existent; follow the course of Fell Beck upstream for several hundred yards, then strike for the depression between Simon Fell and Ingleborough.' Heather still grew on the dry ridges.

Ingleborough's blueness is only a temporary phase, an effect of the atmospheric conditions. A cornflower blue is sometimes observed in summer. At sundown, a walker on the pavement near Southerscales sees a pink hill and the limestone is bathed in a golden light. Blue-greyness is apparent on the northern slopes in winter, even when the hill is plated with snow and ice, for the shadows which creep about the northern side are blue.

Ingleborough is a hollow mountain, with over five hundred feet of limestone, fissured and eroded into a fabulous system of potholes and caves. A few thorn or ash trees which rooted in the grykes are heard wheezing like asthmatic old men when teased by the wind. Woodland in Clapdale gives way, in an acidic area just above the lake, to groves of rhododendrons, even bamboos.

In the dry old woodland, a woodcock, mute and immobile, squats on a clutch of eggs laid on the leaf-litter and, at dusk, her mate circles the territory—a process known as roding—occasionally uttering three grunts and a squeak. One of the Ingleborough gamekeepers showed me three woodcock nests in a single springtime. So closely did they sit, relying on immobility and a cryptic colouration, that through binoculars I could see little more than the sparkle in their eyes.

When I climbed Ingleborough in Coronation Year, 1953, the hill was so dry the vegetation crackled underfoot. I ate my sandwiches in the lee of a crosswall which the Ingleton Fell Rescue Team had made as a commemorative windbreak. The Ingleborough flora is distinguished by ferns but I was unprepared for the sight of an aspidistra protruding from a cavity on the indicator. A note, signed 'Gracie Fields', claimed this plant to be the 'highest aspidistra in the world.'

The summit plateau of Ingleborough, 2,373 ft above sea level, is an area where plants root deeply and keep their heads down. Forty years ago, the idea for the windbreak came from Reg Hainsworth, of Ingleton, who is now ninety years of age. In charge of its construction was Andrew Brown. Both were aware that they must not use stones from the hilltop in case they disturbed what remains of a Brigantean hill-fort.

I found the heap of stones where, in the summer of 1839, a tower or hospice was built and vandalised. The tower was constructed on the instructions of Hornby Roughsedge, a mill-owner at Bentham who had purchased the Manor of Ingleton from the Parker family of Browsholme and was anxious to celebrate his new status.

An account of Mr Roughsedge's vainglorious project was preserved for years by the Kilburns, of the *Hill Inn.* It relates that the opening ceremony took place on a summer's day. 'Races and athletic sports were indulged in. The chief race, twice round the top—about two miles—was won by colliers from Clapham and Ingleton.'

Provisions and liquid cheer had been transported to the hilltop. Elements of the crowd became drunk and unruly, so that when Mr Roughsedge, Mr Overton and other gentlemen had left, discontent between two gangs led to windows and furniture of the new tower being smashed.

'Ornamental coping stones were thrown down. Before darkness fell, much damage had been done. In a few years, the dome was ruthlessly let down by some imp of mischief. This completed the ruin which lies a heap of stones near the south-west corner of the mountain's edge...'

For the 1953 windbreak-cum-indicator, cement and sand were conveyed from Ingleton to Crina Bottom by vehicle and trailer. Stalwarts with redundant rucksacks slogged up the thousand feet of the Yoredales to the hilltop, each carrying 56 lb of material. Jim Sutcliffe, a farmer at Newby, took advantage of the dry spell to drive a tractor and trailer to the summit, via Cod Bank.

The pyramidical bonfire, composed of two hundred and fifty used tyres, with other combustibles, was guarded overnight by Cliff Humphries and Arthur Salter. On Coronation Day, the Rev H J Croft dedicated the windbreak and Mrs Violet Farrer unveiled the view indicator.

Ingleborough lived up to its tradition as a beacon hill when the golden jubilee of Queen Victoria was celebrated in 1887. Herbert Waddington, of Leeds, attended the 'big burn' of ten tons of combustibles, which was witnessed by sixty-one people. They also saw 'rocket signals' from Coniston Old Man and the glow of bonfires on Helvellyn, Skiddaw, Scawfell and the Langdales. Fires blazed on Pendle and Long Preston Moor.

Herbert spent the night on Ingleborough, during which the beacon fires went out, one by one, leaving him—as he put it—'in sole control of the Ingleborough plateau, awaiting, in the eerie darkness of the night, for the coming of dawn.'

Members of the Gritstone Club had an annual trek from the *Hill Inn* to the summit of Ingleborough each Plot Night [November 5]. They carried wood and fuel for a bonfire, the flames from which were seen for miles around.

The triangular summit of the hill, high above the level of the Sands of Morecambe Bay, which are normally in view, is a playground of 'lazy' winds, those intent on blowing straight through you rather than taking the trouble to go round. John Ruskin, who said you might lean on a Yorkshire breeze as you might on a quickthorn hedge, travelled up Chapel-le-Dale when there was 'a bit of a blaw' and marvelled that Ingleborough, so lofty and isolated, was able to stand without rocking.

Reginald Farrer commented on the intense fury of the westerlies coming through the wide gap of Morecambe Bay. 'Even the high, stout walls of the Craven Nursery at Clapham did not break the spirit of those westerly winds.'

Ingleborough, one of a famous trio of hills at the south-west corner of the Yorkshire Dales National Park, had a strong appeal to A J Brown, who wrote: 'Like most Yorkshiremen, I was taught in my boyhood to regard Ingleborough as a sort of Everest. Long before I knew anything about mountaineering (or geography) it was pointed out to me from homely hill-tops as the king of the northern peaks, looming over the further fells like a giant among a swarm of pigmies. . .'

Ingleborough is buttressed by Simon Fell, Park Fell, Southerscales Fell and Little Ingleborough. The massif sprawls over twenty square miles. The finest views are from Chapel-le-Dale.

On the map, Ingleborough has a thin scattering of names. Keld Bank is associated with a spring, Borrins Moor with a heap of stones [an early form of waymarking] and Brunt Rigg was presumably the 'burnt ridge'. The term 'lot' as in High Lot refers to Allotment, a land division at the time of the Enclosures. On the tithe map of the second quarter of last century the full name 'Allotment' is given.

J B Priestley's favourite vantage point was from near the shooting hut at Newby Head. Working quickly, with acrylic paints, he fixed the image of a dove-grey Ingleborough with Park Fell as its attendant. He rejoiced in the hill's clear-cut, simple form—a delight for an impetuous artist.

Farrer, impressed by its isolation and how it formed a rough triangle, wrote in *Blackwood's Magazine* (1908): 'On this great triangle, as on a pedestal, stands the mass of Ingleborough, built, like his two neighbours, of shale and grit, with one narrow belt of mountain limestone appearing about a hundred feet from the summit in an abrupt cliff, on which grow the rare plants for which the hill is celebrated.'

Ingleborough's magnificent girdle of limestone, at an elevation of about 1,000 ft., is unsurpassed in England for its beauty and scientific interest. The limestone is almost pure, fine-grained, either cream of pale grey in hue but weathering to a gleaming white. In places, a limestone pavement is flat and smooth. Elsewhere, the walker uses the clints [blocks] like stepping stones and is wary of slipping into one of the grykes [widened joints].

The other great feature is the abundance of caves and potholes, the latter being the big open rifts. Water from Ingleborough's high shaly ridge courses on to the limestone plateaux and, descending through fissures, re-emerges at the base of the limestone in a dale carved out by glacial ice, being deep enough for grand cave development. In some underground systems, the streams are active and the enlargement of the systems continues. In other caves, dry passages remain, abandoned by watercourses which found lower levels.

Those who explore the Ingleborough underworld are known as

Alum Pot, near Selside.

potholers. Many years ago, sitting in a *Pennine* bus at Settle, I watched a young lad embark with a coil of rope ladder and a metal helmet, Army style. A grizzle-grey passenger asked: 'Are you one o' these pothoiler chaps?' The young man nodded, whereupon the passenger, sighing, remarked: 'Doesn't ta think thou'll spend enuff time below t'grund wi'out going thear now?'

I know of only one man-made cave—a short level, driven through living rock by some long forgotten miner. As I cross Lead

Mine Moss in misty conditions, my imagination takes over. A clink made by a stone displaced by a sheep becomes the sound of a miner's pick against rock. What at first glance looks like a gargantuan snail resolves itself into two distinct boulders.

It is no wonder that the first tourists—those 'gentlemen of taste and leisure' who were out and about towards the end of the eighteenth century—felt shivers passing down their spines when they beheld the strange lunar-type landscape of the pavements. At the mouth of a popular large cave, like Yordas in Kingsdale, the voices of the visitors would reverberate, rousing every echo.

Within the cave, the tourists were at the mercy of the guide who, with his lanthorn flickering, was adept at making their flesh creep with strange tales of the underworld—of boggarts and the shrivelled bodies of those who crept into such natural shelter and died.

Reaching the fretted lip of a pothole, such as Meregill Hole, Long Kin Pot or Gaping Gill, an early tourist would be told these shafts were vents through which water poured at the time of the Flood. They remained (conveniently) in case the Good Lord decided to punish humankind by again flooding the earth.

It was left to the Yorkshire Ramblers' Club, stimulated by Martel's solo descent of Gaping Gill, and blending ingenuity with bravado, to explore most of the big open shafts such as Long Kin West (320 ft deep), which is streamless. In contrast, Alum Pot, on the fell near Selside, swallows a brawling beck which subsequently flows under the River Ribble—a feat made possible by a bed of glacial clay—to re-appear in a pool and flow into the river from the side opposite its source.

In 1856, a geological party set off from the hamlet of Selside, in North Ribblesdale, 'where a guide could be picked up for the sum of 2s who would conduct to many wonderful places. . . Indeed, the whole of the base of Ingleborough contains a world of wonders.'

The Farrer family will come repeatedly into the story of Ingleborough. The family's territorial possessions began with shrewd purchases of land in the eighteenth century. When, early last century, one of the Farrer employees broke through a stalagmatic barrier at the end of a short cave which had been known for ages, access was gained to a passage extending towards the heart of the hill.

Adam Sedgwick, the Dent man who became Woodwardian Professor of Geology at Cambridge, recalled that the passage was generally roomy but in places 'we were forced to use our abdominal muscles as sledges and our mouths as candlesticks.'

John Birkbeck, of Anley, Settle, a pioneer potholer, dated his interest in the underworld from autumn, 1838, when he was taken through the cave and swam across Lake Avernus by candlelight.

Ingleborough Cave, a gash at the base of a 100 ft cliff, became the only underground system to have its ramifications shown on an Ordnance Survey map. One of the Farrer family of Clapham married the Major General who was in charge of the first Survey and he could not resist including the cave, despite a golden rule that only surface details should be included.

Harry Harrison, who guided visitors into Ingleborough Cave early this century, was a poet with a captive audience. He would recite interminably and was not above offering printed versions of his work for sale. Arnold Brown, the guide I knew well, played a tune on some of the stalactites, using the large key of the cave.

Ingleborough Estate have about one third of the hill. The manor and the parish have virtually the same bounds. The presiding Farrer is also lord of the manor of Newby, which is divided into High and Low Divisions and goes up to Newby Head, on the watershed. It takes in only a little of the summit, which otherwise falls within the manor of Ingleton.

John Hutton, the eighteenth century parson who wrote the first book about caves, noted: 'The top of Ingleborough is the first land...that sailors descry in their voyage from Dublin to Lancaster, though above thirty miles from the sea, which shews the great elevation of this mountain.' He had a laborious climb, but towards the end of the nineteeth century Harry Speight, the topographer, was sauntering blithely up the hill with a snack meal he referred to as his 'pocket-dinner'.

Ruskin, who visited the area in the spring of 1859, described the landscape as 'larger in scale and beautifully rustic—wild walls everywhere—moss, crag and mist, wilder than in the Highlands.' He wrote of 'a wind blowing over the whole that seemed as if it would blow Ingleborough into Lancaster Bay. I got out at the top of the moors as the horses were feeding, just to feel what the wind was, and walked backwards and forwards for half an hour, and felt the better for it. I should think I have air enough to last me six months, at least.'

During my long years at *The Dalesman* in Clapham, I was always conscious of being in the shadow of Ingleborough. If nothing else reminded me of it, there were visitors who had just descended from the hill—Professor Joad (he who prefaced his utterances on the radio Brains Trust with the words: 'It all depends what you mean by...') and Graham Watson, complete with ice axe, revelling in some winter walking and with tales to relate of his father's prowess on the crags of Lakeland and the Dales.

The affable Godfrey Wilson, an artist working with pencil or Indian ink, left thoughtful studies of caves and potholes on Ingleborough. When he did work for *The Dalesman,* he jotted down the ideas with the stub of a pencil on the back of an envelope. Both he and Harry Scott clouded the air with pipe smoke.

Another notable artist, Jos Armitage (Ionicus) called to see us after sketching some of the caves for *Punch.* Subsequently, for sixteen years, he painted our cover pictures with such detail that one reader wrote to point out that in a room packed with objects he had forgotten—the door latch.

The most dedicated group of Ingleborough-worshippers included Reg Hainsworth. For many years, summer and winter alike, they left Ingleton at a specific time in the early evening to climb Ingleborough and return so as to be in time for Bill Hind to catch the last bus to Bentham.

On dark nights, they carried torches. They knew Old Ingleborough so well, it was not often that a torch was needed.

Windbreak on Ingleborough.

PART 1

The Natural Scene

> The mass of fells south of the upper waters of the Ure forms Craven, with its well-known cluster of high peaks, Whernside, Ingleborough, Penyghent and Fountains Fell.
>
> *Arthur Raistrick, 1968.*

> Here is the finest series of limestone pavements in Britain.
>
> *Peter Corkhill, speaking at the opening of the Ingleborough Nature Reserve in 1993.*

> The dramatic scenery of Ingleborough changes from a vast network of underground caverns, through an area of limestone pasture, meadow and woodland, to vegetation adapted to the harsher conditions of higher altitudes.
>
> *Leaflet issued by English Nature.*

Studying the Rocks

THE GEOLOGY of Ingleborough (2,373 ft) can be simply expressed. Just think of a sandwich cake, with well-defined horizontal layers. In the case of Ingleborough, the layers represent different types of rock. These have been subjected to differential weathering. This hill, like its neighbours, has a stepped appearance.

Almost all the visible rocks are of the Carboniferous Age, between 360 and 290 million years old. The rocks were originally sediments which accumulated in sea, swamp and delta. They rest on the impermeable strata of Silurian, Ordovician and Pre-Cambrian rocks which are up to 500 million years old. Slates of Ordovician age occur between Austwick and Clapham, with a large outcrop visible at the head of Ingleborough Lake in Clapdale. The oldest rocks are the Pre-Cambrian strata, exposed near Ingleton.

The Great Scar Limestone, over 500 ft of remarkably pure rock, is composed of the skeletal remains of small sea creatures—coral, crinoids and bryozoans—which abounded in a clear warm sea, bright with corals. Pick up a piece of limestone and you may see the petrified remains of this ancient life. Albert Mitchell went a stage further and wrote: 'You may strike the solid rock with a hammer and immediately the percussion liberates a peculiar kerosene-like odour which tells of the old animal oils in which the limestone is steeped.'

Rising from the limestone are the Yoredale Series, a rhythmic succession of bands of limestone, along with layers of shale and grit. This strata gives Ingleborough its step-geology. The Yoredales, which were laid down as marine sediments, were so-named by John Phillips (1833), who studied them in Yoredale [Wensleydale].

Reginald Farrer, commenting on the stepped beds of the Yoredales which rise sheerly from a broad limestone base, compared the hill proper to a statue with an extra large plinth. 'Splendid as are the proportions of Ingleborough, the pavement of limestone spreads out far and wide beneath the last steep slopes of the gritstone giant himself, so that on surmounting the lower fells one finds oneself on a perfectly flat even floor of white boulders stretching away to the foot of the mountain.'

Ingleborough's weather-resistant cap is about 50 ft of the lowest bed of the Millstone Grit, so named because its coarseness made it suitable for millstones. It did not over-heat the grain. The Grit has been worn down to a plateau.

The south-west extent of the Ingleborough massif is marked by the Craven Fault, a vertical cracking of the strata which resulted in a drop of over 5,000 ft to the south. The downthrow is graphically illustrated at Ingleton where coal mined at a depth of 1,000 ft was originally connected with a seam long since eroded from near the summit of Ingleborough.

Ingleton church has an unstable situation on the fault line. A former Vicar exaggerated wildly when he told me, as a joke, that Ingleton was originally built on the summit of Ingleborough and descended en bloc as the fault developed.

Minor faults, joints and beddings in the limestone permitted water to enter. Rainwater, becoming a weak solution of acid through contact with the atmosphere and vegetation, began a process of erosion which has honeycombed Ingleborough with potholes and caves.

These have been enlarged by torrents bearing grit in suspension and by the abrasive quality of pebbles swirled round and round by the force of a stream so that circular holes were created, the holes eventually merging.

In what Arthur Raistrick grandly called 'the Great Ice Age of the Pleistocene period', glaciers over-rode all but the highest hills. Ingleborough itself was smothered in ice during the last (Devensian) glaciation. Then, as the ice began to retreat, there was a period when the hill, with its smooth new lines, was a nunatak [a peak which rose above the surrounding ice, the centre of dispersal being a little to the north].

Glaciers deepened into troughs the old river valleys and smeared the slopes of Ingleborough and its neighbours with a mush we call boulder-clay. The smoother slopes on the flanks of Ingleborough are where the rock has been plastered with this glacial drift.

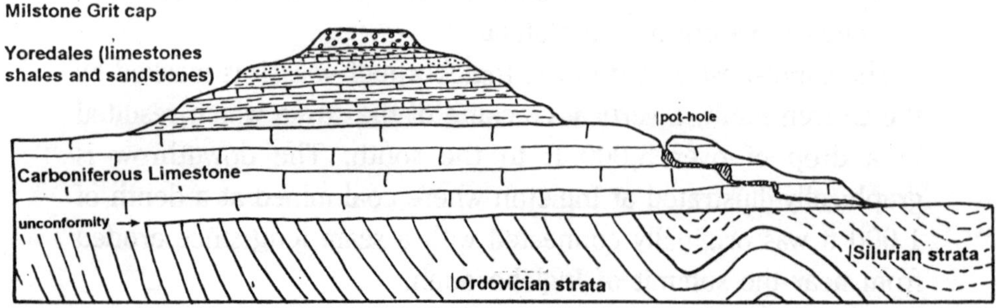

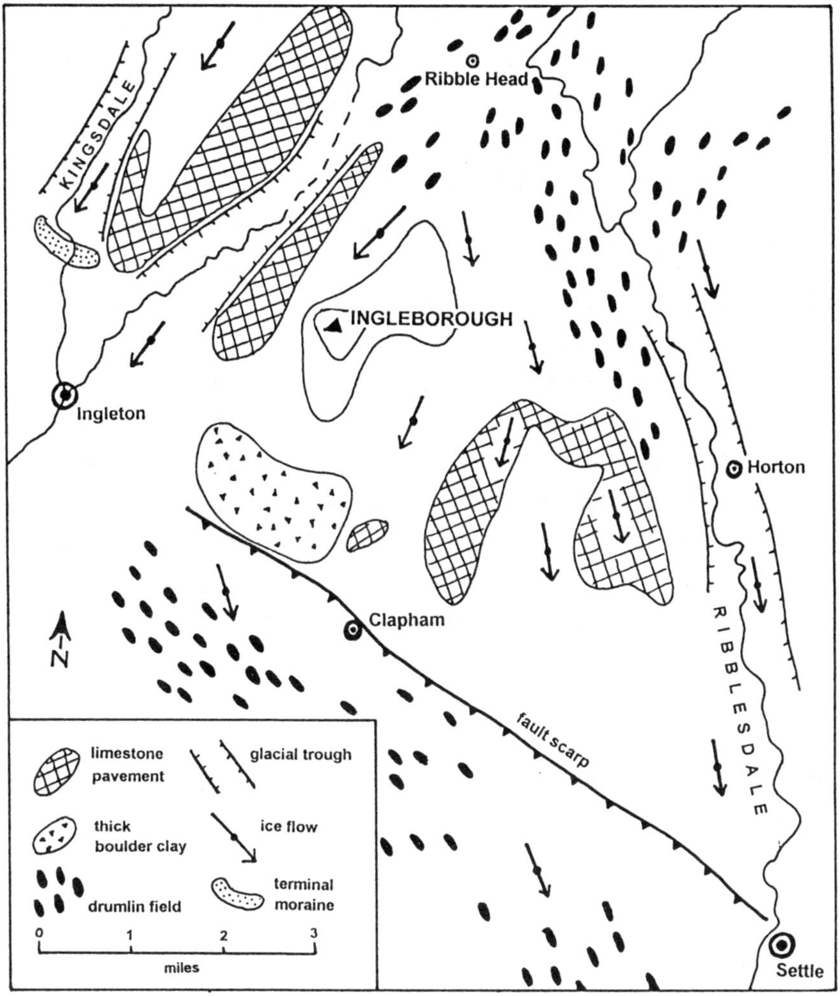

Glaciation of Ingleborough.

The Crummackdale glacier, active about 11,000 years ago, broke off large pieces of Silurian rock and shifted them about half a mile, where they came to rest on limestone as so-called erratics. Erratics could have occurred, according to Fred Hoyle, by rocks skidding along the top of the ice field.

In the intervening years, weathering of the limestone round about a piece of rock, but not of the rock immediately below the Silurian boulders, left the foreign boulders resting on pedestals of limestone.

Water which fell as rain on the gritstone cap of Ingleborough and which takes its slow and complex course through the limestone, emerges (as already mentioned) above the impervious slate. Farrer, in his vivid style, wrote: 'For in his magnificent solitude, Ingleborough gathers all the clouds of heaven, and their rains streaming down his slopes have so fretted away the limestone of the levels that, here and there, the waters disappear into some secret chink or narrow terrible shaft between the rocks...'

The Yorkshire Geological Society, keen to trace the subterranean waters, used pack horses with salt about the time of the 1914-18 war. Much later, a harmless green dye known as fluorescein was introduced to a watercourse above Crina Bottom. The water entered the White Scar system (then unknown) and flowed into Ingleton reservoir.

It is related that when the scientists returned to their lodgings and turned on the taps, what looked like pea soup gushed forth...

Ingleborough in Flower

THE HIGH crags of The Ark, on Ingleborough, were the hunting ground of plant-collectors from the time of John Ray, who travelled this way on horseback in 1677, and jotted down the first English record of the purple saxifrage (*Saxifraga oppositifolia*).

Ray found the plant 'on the North side of Ingleborough hill, near a bog by the side of an underground river.' Did he really 'find' it unaided? It is known that Thomas Willisel, an old soldier, who had botanically combed the Ingleborough and Settle areas, showed the great naturalist several rare plants, including the purple saxifrage.

Tom Hey, an old friend of mine, suggested that the purple saxifrage should be re-named 'Ingleborough Beauty'. The flower, a relic from the period immediately after the Ice Age, blooms virtually unseen at its cliff haunts high on the hill but is familiar to many people, having been introduced to the garden rockery.

Reginald Farrer exulted in its presence in high places. '*Oppositifolia* is a native of our limestone cliffs about 2,000 ft up, and forms great sheets of colour in early April on Ingleborough and Penyghent. It varies in depth of tone, and there is one most ardent crimson one who sits secure on an inaccessible precipice of Penyghent.'

Farrer's specific reference was to a form with frail-growing crimson flowers, finer even than the advertised splendens which Tom Hey collected on Ingleborough and thought of as *splendidissima* —the name being an example, he said, of the Farrer exuberance bubbling to the surface. I have seen the 'Ingleborough Beauty' flowering in March, at a time when the hill was powdered white with snow. The flowers of this alpine plant were attracting bees.

After Ray's time, the avarice of collectors prompted Harry Speight, the Victorian topographer, to call them 'the hamper men'. It was shameful, he said, that the rarer plants and ferns were being sold 'only to perish in the impure atmosphere of towns, thus robbing the mountain of one of its great natural charms.'

Among the happy hunters of unusual plants (let it be whispered) was Farrer, though he probably did not include among his booty the bird's eye primrose (*Primula farinosa*), which he adored, commenting that the 'mountain-masses of Ingleborough' is the centre of its distribution.

All through the winter, nothing was to be seen but a round, fat bud. 'Then, with spring, unfold the mealy little grey leaves, in themselves a joy.' When June arrived, 'up go the white stems, and out come the semi-globular trusses of lovely pink, golden-eyed flowers, looking so sweet and friendly there is no resisting them.'

My introduction to botanical Ingleborough came through Chris Cheetham, a confirmed bachelor, born in 1875, the year which also saw the inception of the Yorkshire Naturalists' Union. Chris, a refugee from the family textile business, settled in Austwick in 1934 and reverted to nature. He did not shave and, except in the bitterest winter, he wore shorts instead of long trousers.

Chris was an all-round naturalist, an authority on moss and lichen. He ate most kinds of fungi and when I went out with him he was continually handing me the leaf of this plant and that plant with the remark: 'Chew this. What does it taste like?' I can still taste the cucumber-like flavour of salad burnet.

It was a joy to visit the home of one of the last of the Victorian naturalists and look through his microscope. A species of daddy-longlegs was named after him—*Tipula Cheethami.* Some specimens in his collection of two-winged flies were minute. It was Chris who showed me some of the arctic-alpine plants on the Yoredale limestone band, at an elevation of between 2,150 ft and 2,200 ft. We viewed them through binoculars; they were happily—for their own good—out of reach of both man and sheep.

On Ingleborough grows Herb Christopher (baneberry). Geoffrey Grigson, who wrote charmingly about our English floral heritage, and described the skirts and slopes of the hill as 'crumbly and floriferous', noted that 'around Ingleborough this plant fills hole after hole between the grey chunks of limestone, or in the grey clefts between the limestone pavements.'

Here bloom yellow mountain saxifrage (*Saxigrara aizoides*) and mossy saxifrage (*Saxifrago hynoides*), which sports cream flowers. Up there, where mist often hangs about like a damp shroud, is hoary whitlowgrass (*Draba incana*), brittle bladder fern (*Cystopteris fragilis*) and green spleenwort (*Aspienium viride*). The alpine clubmoss has not been recorded for many years, though Ingleborough is still a haven for woolly fringe moss and the upright clubmoss.

A plant growing high on Ingleborough must cope with extremes of temperature, with heavy rainfall and strong winds. The precipitation on Ingleborough must be considerably more than the average of seventy inches a year noted at Ribblehead, but Ingleborough is not a conspicuously wet hill. The run-off is swift.

The summit vegetation, apart from a hardy sedge, has been virtually trampled out in recent years. As mentioned, the limestone cliffs around the rim are floriferous. To list them all would be to invite writer's cramp. Roseroot sports its yellow flowers in May and June. Alpine saw-wort (*Saussurea alpina*), which is more commonly found in Lakeland's wet gullies, maintains a precarious hold.

A diminutive form of lady's mantle (*Alchemila minima*), found only in the Ingleborough area, appears to have been successful because it can cope with close grazing of the turf by sheep.

Cloudberry (*Rubus chamaemorus*) maintains its grip on a cheerless, peaty terrain. It fruits in mid-July, the berry turning yellow when ripe. The sixteenth century botanist Gerard recorded that cloudberry grew profusely 'on Mount Ingleborrow the highest in all England', and was thus named because it occurred 'where the clouds are lower than the tops [of the hills] all winter long.'

It is a pretty story. Geoffrey Grigson—he who referred to Ingleborough's 'wild garden of streams and natural sculpture and flowers'—gently debunked the idea, stating that the name cloudberry means 'hill berry', from the Old English *clud,* for hill.

Farrer wrote: 'The fruit is its great attraction. The plant is about six inches in height, with two or three rounded leaves, blackcurrant-like, thick and solid. The big white flower stands solitary at the top of the stem, staring upwards. And there, in time, forms the fruit, ripening about August—an enormous raspberry of fewer and larger carpels, russet-red at first, then ripening to a soft, golden amber—when its taste has the sparkling acidity of the Pomegranate. Unfortunately, the grouse share my love for its juices...'

On Simon Fell, the peat hags—created in the wet sub-Atlantic period—are now diminishing. The peat formed rapidly, overwhelming the native forest and preserving much of it in its claggy wetness. Now, many centuries later, following hard grazing by sheep and the freeze-thaw effect of winter weather, it is unlikely these peatlands will recover. 'Frost-heave' puffs up the peat. As soon as it dries out, the wind blows the disturbed material away.

The wind has also brought acid rain. Last century, when the textile industry throve in Lancashire, and every town was dominated by a forest of smoking mill chimneys, the prevailing south-west wind carried pollution to Ingleborough and its Pennine neighbours.

In our botanical progress, descending Ingleborough, we reach the acidic grits and shales of the Yoredale Series, known as the 'bilberry edge', because the soil, being free-draining, its nutrients leached out, has bilberry as the natural climax plant.

The area below the scarp was scrub, as evidenced by pieces of birch and, to a lesser extent, rowan recovered from the peat on places like High Lot and South House Moor. Within living memory, the drier ground had a thick cover of heather, giving the hill a purple hue in late summer.

Sheep, grouse and heather co-existed on a well-managed hill. Both creatures liked their heather young. The browsing by sheep trimmed the heather. That which grew rank [overgrown] at about seven years was swizzened [systematically burned by the gamekeepers]. The heather had usually re-established itself by the

Ingleborough from Crina Bottom.

following summer and the sheep dined on it until its useful period ended in about February.

Then cotton sedge took up the running. Hill ewes hunted out the flower buds in what was known to the Pennine farmer as 'mosscrop'. A sheep delicately plucked out a bud with a length of white stem attached.

During the 1939-45 war, when it was vital to grow more food, the sheep population began a dramatic increase. Sheep subsidy led to more and more sheep and to overgrazing, the demise of the heather and its replacement by unpalatable grasses, such as *Nardus stricta,* which is low in nutrition, quite apart from being disliked by the sheep. Dr John Farrer calls it 'sheep-resistant grass'.

Contrast this dull, tussocky land with the few traditional hay meadows around the foot of Ingleborough, where traditional management is restoring the variety of plants seen before the use of artificial fertilisers were introduced to increase the grass yield.

A limestone pasture, though closely cropped by sheep, can be a delight to the botanist, the flowering plants including bird's eye primrose, thyme and yellow mountain pansy.

Visiting botanists remember with special clarity Ingleborough's world-famous limestone pavements. The moonscape effect of clints and grykes may be a recent phenomenon. In prehistoric times, large areas were probably covered with soil. Heavy stocking and poaching [laceration caused by trampling by stock] would soon affect a change.

The pavements vary in appearance. Some are low, comprised of large flat slabs, which are slippery to the foot when wet, and others are today raised above the surrounding ground and have ankle-ricking grykes. Ingleborough Common is heavily grazed while Colt Park Wood (purchased by the old Nature Conservancy in 1959) may never have been grazed because it is inherently dangerous to stock and the boundary walls have been well maintained.

In this case, 'park' simply means an enclosure. The plants which find shelter and moisture in the grykes include many with a woodland association. A dominant plant in limestone habitat is the blue moor grass, common enough on Ingleborough but rare in a national context. Grykes in a pavement support some of the less common ferns, like the rigid buckler and the limestone polypody.

Yorkshire sandwort (*Arenaria gothica*), with its white flower, is a subspecies found only in the Ingleborough area. The plant was first identified at Ribblehead station in 1889. Reginald Farrer, aged fourteen, submitted a report to the *Journal of Botany* about finding the plant on Ingleborough.

Today, the annual census of the Yorkshire sandwort reveals the presence of about 2,000 plants. The year 1993, characterised by a wet springtime, was so good for it that the number of plants recorded was double the average figure and seed was collected for the National Seed Bank.

The rare Teesdale violet is a difficult plant to spot on Ingleborough, being a pale violet in hue. Normally, non-flowering plants are found, being identified by the leaves and the number of hairs on the stem.

Colt Park, the aboriginal ash wood already mentioned, was described by the botanist J E Lousley in *Flowers of the Chalk and Limestone* as 'one of the most remarkable and uncanny in Britain'. Whereas the vegetation on a limestone pavement is restricted, by the grazing of animals, to the grykes, Colt Park's woodland situation affords shelter and greater humidity, stimulating the growth of mosses and lichen on the rock.

In summer, the cracks and crannies are disguised by lush growth. Here grows the yellow Star of Bethlehem, Angular Solomon's Seal, Lesser Prickly Sedge, Northern Hawksbeard, Herb Paris, Baneberry, Lily of the Valley—to mention a few of the 230 species of flowering plants recorded here.

The Lune and Ribble valleys open their mouths to the mild breezes of Morecambe Bay. There is a laggard spring in the upper valleys—in Chapel-le-Dale and North Ribblesdale—but in due course the earth warms, the first flush of grass appears and with it showy flowering plants. The meadows and pastures which have not been drenched with modern fertilisers yield primrose, cowslip, mayflower, ox-eye daisy, buttercup, common orchid, mayflower and harebell.

The wind which howls across Ingleborough inhibits tree growth. Those ash trees at Colt Park may be only 20 feet tall but have an age in excess of 300 years. Concern about this natural wood led to the repeat of a survey of the trees first carried out 30 years ago. It was assessed there are rather more trees now than before. Young trees are protected by man-made devices against the gnawing of hungry rabbits.

English Nature has earmarked an area where small exclosures

of indigenous ash have been planted and the area left to itself. Tree plots have been created in one or two of the gills to restore fragments of the old mixed type of woodland.

Hardly any native woodland remains in the Clapham area. Woods like Sunnybank and Wood Meadow were planted by the Farrers between the 1820s and the 1920s. Some trees were intended as cover for game birds. They also, incidentally, sheltered farm stock. The Farrers planted to beautify the environs of their home, Ingleborough Hall, and the old drive was edged by copper beeches which are from seventy to ninety years old.

The characteristic trees in the village are foliage trees—cherry, almond, whitebeam, many of them being planted by Roland Farrer, who was a sheep farmer in New Zealand before taking over the estate. I remember him as a man roughened by years of hard work in the pioneering days 'down under'. The older trees in the village—sycamore, a few beeches and chestnuts, with a sprinkling of limes—are from 120 to 140 years old.

Rayside, the most elevated wood on the estate, lies on the 1,300 ft contour line and is seen by those who trudge towards Gaping Gill. Rayside represents woodland nearly at the limits of economic tree growth. On the windward side are some Scots pines. The rest is a mixture of larch, ash and a few sycamore.

They were in marked contrast with the now felled Norway spruce planted by the beck in Clapham Woods. When I first walked this way, using the old carriageway, I looked up to them and was doubly impressed when I realised that a tree was already some forty feet high at the elevation at which I stood.

Birds, Beasts and Butterflies

INGLEBOROUGH is not a particular good hill for birds. The number of species is small. The birds themselves are thinly distributed. The commonest nesting species must be the meadow pipit. In winter, when for most of the time only the honk of a carrion crow breaks the stillness, I look for a cheery flock of snow buntings, refugees from Iceland or other points north, dining on the molinia. The birds, with much white on their plumage, resemble snowflakes when tossed about by the wind.

A raven, sacred bird of the Norse folk, may be seen on the corpse of a sheep which has found the winter too much to bear. Ravens from nests in Lakeland or on the Northern Pennines drift down to winter in the Dales. Their croaking breaks the quietness of high and lonely places.

A pair which nested for years in the Three Peaks Country had eggs to tend when the hill was patched with snow. Once, after a heavy fall, the nest (with its sitting bird) was the only dark object in view. I recall the alertness of the raven. Its voice was heard long before I reached the nesting area and it put on a flying display, flicking upside down, then back again.

The raven then settled at the edge of the nesting crag and used up surplus nervous energy by tugging out pieces of grass and tossing them to the Pennine breeze. Another raven, viewed above Crummackdale, turned on its back and flew upside down for a considerable distance.

The peregrine falcon, now relatively common, does not (as far as I know) nest on the Ingleborough cliffs. I have never heard the chatter of annoyance nor seen the distinctive crossbow silhouette of a disturbed bird whenever I have walked around the rim of the hill.

In late spring, there is just a chance of seeing a trip [small party] of dotterel, one of the rarest species in Britain, on passage from the wintering grounds near the Mediterranean to the high, snow-rimmed mountains of the northern lands.

The clear whistle of a golden plover is heard on Ingleborough, where in most years only a single pair may be nesting. In August, however, a moderately large number of golden plover converge on soft ground near Sulber Nick and join the lapwings in feeding on invertebrates such as leather jackets. I have seen a vagrant dunlin (the so-called plover's page) on Ingleborough, but dunlin favour the wetter hills, especially where there is some standing water, as with a peaty tarn.

The red grouse, a stocky bird with rufous-brown plumage, is scarce. The loss of the heather removed the grouse's staple food. South House Moor (now part of the nature reserve) was considered to be the best grouse area by the sporty set.

The lapwing, with its tufty wings and wispy crest, selects a damp area for nesting. There may be several nests in one area, which local farmers refer to as 'tewit grund' after a Dales name for the bird. In spring and summer, the curlew climbs briskly, arches itself like a feathered kite and drifts earthwards giving its bubbling song. Curlews are less common than they were. And finding a nest on a hillside of Nardus is not the easiest of occupations.

A pair of ring ouzels—white-bibbed 'mountain blackbirds'—have nested in Braithwaite Wife Hole at Southerscales. Another white-bibbed bird, the dipper, was flushed from the funnel-like Gaping Gill. I have seen the bird's mossy nest on a ledge of rock kept permanently wet from the spray of Fell Beck. In the normal beck or riverside setting, a pair of dippers have grey wagtails for company. The last pair of grey wagtails I saw nesting had selected a cliff face site in Trow Gill.

Wheatears chack and whistle where there are rock outcrops. Some pairs nest in old rabbit burrows. At a time of tree-felling in

Curlews return to Ingleborough.

Clapham Woods, I photographed blackbirds which were nesting on the ground, beside a fallen giant and among the litter of last year's leaves.

Tawny owls find the woodland attractive. The night air shivers with the hooting of the male and the *kewick* of the female. Mixed flocks of tits, sometimes with a tree creeper in train, give a sense of life to the winter woodland.

The redstart, also known as firetail, inhabits fragements of old woodland. The wood warbler may be heard in Colt Park.

Of the Ingleborough mammals, by far the commonest is the sheep, either Dalesbred or Swaledale. Mrs Farrer, mother of Reginald, kept a footloose flock of Jacob's sheep which, if not at the Home Farm, were usually to be found near Trow Gill.

Goats owned by a farmer at Newby Cote also made for this area. In the spring of the year, when the goats had kidded and there was a good flow of milk, the farmers rounded up their animals and had them ready in case a ewe had dried up or lambs had been orphaned. Rob Hird recalls the boyhood experience of walking from Newby Cote looking for goats and finding them in Trow Gill, where he had the task of driving them from the ledges and directing them back to the farm.

The roe deer is well-established in quiet tracts of woodland and has also been seen on the high, exposed Park Fell. Clapham Woods and the Ingleton Glens were once the resort of red squirrels.

Ingleborough is not ideal country for brown hares, but some are present. Rabbits scutter about the thinly wooded areas and heaps of dross in old quarries. Ingleborough was the home of thousands of rabbits, many of them perishing in a bad winter. In the early months of 1947, when the hill was white over for weeks on end, large numbers of rabbits—'all skin and bone'—appeared at the farms

Moles burrow through the easily-worked soil of the limestone areas. Tot Lord, of Settle, who was ever alert for traces of early human activity, had a dibber fixed to the end of his walking stick and with its help he disturbed mole heaps, hoping that the industrious animals had thrown up some flints used by Early Man.

Foxes are relatively common. The Lunesdale pack of hounds arrives in the district now and again but in most cases foxes are shot, without ceremony. The wily native foxes lay up on The Arks and, being few in number, did not cause much trouble. In recent times, foxes gathered up in urban areas have been released in rural areas, including Ingleborough. 'These foxes are not used to going to ground. They sleep out on top and are bad to get.'

Badgers operate at elevations of up to 2,000 ft., as evidenced by the sight of scooped-out skins of hedgehogs. A badger which had become stuck when negotiating a cripple or hog hole in a wall on the side of High Lot had throttled itself. Frogs have been found at 2,000 ft. Snails of various species festoon the limestone pavement.

Ingleborough is not the place the layman would associate with butterflies, but a colony of the northern brown argus, which feeds on rock rose and nationally is rare, was discovered in a limestone pavement area. The species is easily overlooked.

The antler moth, of high elevations, periodically occurs at plague proportions. It was such a plague just before the 1914-18 war which attracted black-headed gulls from the coast. Many of them stayed to nest on the Whernside tarns.

At Colt Park, where a moth trap has been used, the species caught included a yellow-winged carpet, known from only one other site in Yorkshire. The specimen of thyme pug [the caterpillar feeds on thyme] was another valuable record for Ingleborough. The brindled ochre caterpillar feeds on the roots of angelica. Because it flies in April and October, and the females hibernate through the winter, it has been overlooked. Now it is recognised as a moth regularly present on the hill.

The cave spider found in the Ingleborough systems is not an albino, as you might suppose from its residence in caves. This species is black and shiny, the male being extremely large. The egg mass, which is pear-shaped, hangs from a cave roof.

PART 2

History and Folklore

The First Settlers

IF MAN lived on or around Ingleborough before the Ice Age, then no traces of him have been found. What we do have is evidence of human habitation spanning some 5,000 years.

The archaeologist Alan King says of what he terms the central Pennine limestone province: 'It is as densely covered today with freestanding archaeological monuments as any part of the southern English chalklands. This evidence extends from Neolithic cairns and rock shelters to expanses of celtic field systems.'

The story of human activity begins with the hunter-gatherers of the late upper Palaeolithic age to whom the limestone caves formed constricted but useful shelter. For a millenium, the human visitors to the hill and its flanking valleys flitted like shadows through an area lightly covered with woodland—with ash, hazel and birch. The Mesolithic period (800-4000 BC) saw the beginnings of what was to be man's devastating mark on the landscape.

His domesticated animals, or perhaps even the herding of deer, meant there was no regeneration of timber.

Neolithic folk (4000-1800 BC) were the first real farmers, growing simple crops and keeping stock on the easily-worked, well-drained limestone fringes of Ingleborough. A mixed farming economy was practised, which means that in addition to stock rearing (as now) the early farmers were also engaged in cereal farming.

In Neolithic times, the deforestation, which began in the Mesolithic, accelerated. Long periods of forest clearance took place as man with polished stone axes felled more and more deciduous trees. The destruction of the soils led over an immense period of time to the exposure of those limestone pavements which had not already been cleared of soil by the abrasive action of glacial ice.

Bronze Age settlement (1800-600 BC) has not been extensively identified, but there are numerous Bronze Age burial cairns, indicating that communities continued to farm the Ingleborough massif. When the Celtic culture arrived on the Craven uplands, the local tribe, the Brigantes, enjoyed a good climatic phase, which made settlement on the hills tolerable.

Of the British way of life on and around Ingleborough in Roman times, Alan King observes: 'The picture is for a very thriving arable economy, hemp (the stuff used for ropemaking) being grown in the area immediately below Ingleborough on the north-west flank. . . The spread of early field systems is almost continuous from Ribblehead to Horton or from Ribblehead to Chapel-le-Dale on the limestone, then along the valley floor from this dale to Ingleton.'

Was there a regular habitation on the summit of Ingleborough, where are to be found the remains of a rampart wall and circular huts? These are said to be of Brigantean origin. The story develops against the background of Roman penetration of the north. Cartimandua, the native queen, divorced her husband Venutius and threw in her lot with the Romans.

Venutius led the Brigantean patriots in a defence of their tribal lands. It is said that he gathered some of his best supporters in the Ingleborough area, with the hill-fort as a point of defence. Arthur Raistrick, the Dales antiquary, was among those who were convinced that for a time this hill-fort summit was the capital of the Venutian revolt, though it must have existed for a considerable period before the Roman Conquest. . .

(Sir Mortimer Wheeler thought the last Brigantian stand took place behind huge earthworks at Stanwick, near the Tees, where in 74 AD Roman might triumphed in battle. In due course the Romans drove a road from Bainbridge, by the upper Ure, to Lancaster, the road traversing Chapel-le-Dale).

The Royal Commission's report on the Ingleborough hill-fort refers to the highly-unusual construction of the rampart wall. It consists of a gritstone wall, the rear face formed of orthostatic blocks and the outer face of drystone construction.

The rubble walls of the huts show little variation in size or form. A piece of pottery found on Ingleborough indicates that the hill fort was being used in late Roman times [third or fourth century].

With the spread of the Angles (the Saxons not being found in the North), several English settlements appeared—Ingleton, Thornton, Twistleton being examples. Clapham, an Anglian village, holds a typical site, well sheltered, with a copious supply of fresh water. Traces of terracing on the steep hillside speaks of the need to maximise on arable farming in later times.

The Irish-Norse settlers of over 1,100 years ago settled in scattered farms at the daleheads and occupied the limestone fringe of Ingleborough. Between Park Fell and Ribblehead is an excavated example—the foundations of three buildings with low stone walls of boulders which had supported thatched roofs. One structure was impressively large—sixty feet long and, internally, 12 feet wide. Coins found in this building date from the third quarter of the ninth century.

Alan King, who excavated the site, has pointed out the complexity of the settlement record. Not far from the southern doorway of the long rectangular dwelling rose a burial mound. 'This proved to cover a stone cist, in which lay a leaf-shaped arrowhead: two sites only yards apart, separated by perhaps three thousand years of human activity.'

Until monastic times, the number of sheep was small and the animals shared the big upland grazings with the indigenous red deer, which had been in the area since the climate ameliorated at the close of the Ice Age. Small black cattle and goats were also kept by early farmers.

The sheep triumphed as the monasteries developed a wool trade large enough to meet their ambitions to build splendid abbeys. Ingleborough was shared among several abbeys, the principal being Furness (who had a grange at Newby and Chapel-le-Dale, with outlying pastures at Newby Head, on the watershed between the Ribble and the Ure). Jervaulx owned much land in North Ribblesdale, having a reputation for horse-breeding (hence the name Studfold for the hamlet between Horton, 'horse town', and Helwith).

When the monasteries were dispossessed in the time of Henry VIII, the lands were privatised. Farming did not recover fully until after the Civil War. Then the yeoman families, confident in the settled conditions that their property might be passed down from generation to generation, re-built in stone and slate, thus creating the vernacular style of architecture which is much admired today.

As the better-off families wished to benefit from new ideas of stock-rearing, a movement began to enclose commonland, first by agreement and later—in the eighteenth and nineteenth centuries—by Acts of Parliament, the latter resulting in the now familiar grid-iron pattern of drystone walls. A consequence was the appearance, on the Ingleborough map of The Allotment [a share of the enclosed land].

Ingleborough Common was not enclosed and at Austwick the pastures of Moughton, Oxenber and Long Scar (Ingleborough) though ringed by walls were still used communally, the lord of the manor having the mineral rights but each farm with rights to graze sheep being allocated an appropriate number of stints or gaits. Each represents the pasturage of a single animal. The term 'acre' is of little significance in areas where there is so much unproductive rock.

Hill Farmers

Ingleborough from Chapel-le-Dale.

When Ingleborough wears a hat
The haytime man can take a nap.
Frank Coultherd, of Lodge Bank.

Ingleborough is a good fell for sheep; it's stocked too hard—that's trouble.
A local farmer, 1993.

When my grandfather used to walk from Bleak Bank over to Crina Bottom House, the heather was so thick it was springy underfoot.
Jim Smith, 1993.

THE OLD-TIME farmer set off for the hill with a dog at heel and a few sandwiches to sustain him until evening. Two generations on, and his descendants have all-terrain vehicles. The dog rides pillion. They are back home for lunch.

Despite his high mobility, a farmer on the flanks of Ingleborough still needs all his wits and stamina in the face of a cool climate and thin soils. The winter seems to occupy half the year. The long-established farming families are now as 'heafed' to the hill as the sheep which drank in their love of specific areas with their mother's milk.

Ingleborough weather is cool and cloudy in summer, being fanned by mild breezes from Morecambe Bay, though a breeze may soon become a tumultuous blast and when the snow-dogs from the north-east are howling a visitor to Ingleborough summit has ice crystals in the bloodstream.

Ingleborough has its own personal cloud and draws a lot of rain, but the hill is free-draining. Water bubbling from innumerable springs disappears down fissures in the limestone to reappear above the impermeable slates. A lusty beck forms on the eastern slope and leaps into Gaping Gill. Less conspicuous is the water coursing down Greywife Sike, from Knoutber, adjacent to Little Ingleborough. 'T'watter goes down t'fell and disappears into a pothole.'

John Farrer told me of an arrangement in the 1920s to bring a water supply to the high-lying farms of Clapdale and Flatts, plus a number of fields. It was done by the aid of hydraulic ram pumps, which were attended by the gamekeeper as he went on his rounds.

Know Gap Sike, which extends for miles, once had stretches where earthenware pipes were laid; there was even a trestle bridge. The sike fed water to Clapdale Farm, with a branch—traceable on the older maps—down to Flatts Farm. Though claimed by some to be monastic in origin, the watercourse was probably no more than 200 years old. When it went into disrepair, it was replaced by about four miles of plastic pipe and a score of water troughs, installed with the support of agricultural grants.

As recently as forty years ago, before the sheep population greatly increased, the bonnie heather, murmurous with bees and crackling with the voices of grouse, bloomed over much of

Ingleborough. When most of it had been eaten off, George Murray, gamekeeper on Ingleborough Estate, took the squire to a point just above Bleak Bank Farm, put his heel in the ground and said: 'That's where the heather used to come to.' There was no heather in sight.

The Ingleborough sheep, once a nondescript 'crag sheep', are now Swaledales and Dales-breds. The former emanated when farmers on and around Tan Hill got together to fix a type. The Dales-bred, a type originating in Upper Wharfedale, soon became the major breed of the Craven district.

The evolutionary process provided these northern sheep with the equivalent of coat and waistcoat and an ability to withstand extremes of climate. 'It is more of a Dales-bred country just here,' says a farmer friend. 'They say that Swaledales should never have their feet dry.'

Ingleborough has large tracts of common, notably Ingleborough and Clapham Commons, also the allotment areas, where land was allocated and provided with drystone walls at the time of the Enclosure Acts, in this case early last century. Examples are High Lot, South House Moor and Borrins.

The enclosure of Clapham's common lands began in 1809 with the requisite Act of Parliament but was not put into effect until 1835. The Farrers were the main landowners but about seventy other people were noted as holding stints or having turbary [peat-cutting] rights which had to be protected.

In successive years, other parcels of common land were walled-in and came under private ownership but the steeper slopes on Ingleborough retained their old status of commonland. Such commonland, including Newby Moor [popularly known as Clapham Common] used to extend unbroken across the valley. It was said there was only one gate [at Newby Cote] between the top of Ingleborough and the top of Burnmoor.

A typical hill farm of half a century ago had some inland (meadow and good pastureland of about forty acres) plus grazing rights on an adjacent tract of fell. The farm was run by family labour, augmented by an Irishman at haytime.

Jaded meadowland was fertilised each spring by applications of muck [dung] from the midden which lay beside a barn-cum-shippon in which a few milk cattle were over-wintered. In the period before artificial fertilisers were introduced, haymeadows around Ingleborough were spangled with wild flowers. Now most of them are a uniform green.

Over most of Ingleborough, the hill farmers use their discretion as to how many sheep the land will carry. On the Austwick pastures—which include Long Scar (Ingleborough)—the land is stinted, a stint representing the pasturage of a sheep.

Each local farm has its allocation of stints, which determine how many animals he may graze, and rules which were written in a calf-bound minute book [first entry, 1814] also deal with the times of year when sheep may be grazed and the responsibilities of shepherds (no longer appointed), also such mundane matters as the care of walls and mole-catching.

Meeting each February at the 'herd-letting', the farmers discuss mutual problems. The great days of herd-letting were in the 1930s, when tenders were required from men willing to tend the sheep. Three shepherds were needed. Stock could be put on the pastures on May 15 until August 12.

The pastures were then rested for a short time, to be subsequently stocked with half-gaits until February. A shepherd had to visit his charges once a day 'until the wool is off' [shearing time], when visits were less frequent. When no sheep were being grazed on the big upland pastures, the shepherd applied himself to gap-walling.

Continued on page 57.

Impressions of Ingleborough. *Above:* An engraving of the hill from near Weathercote House by William Westall (1818). *Below:* A view from the limestone pavement near Southerscales.

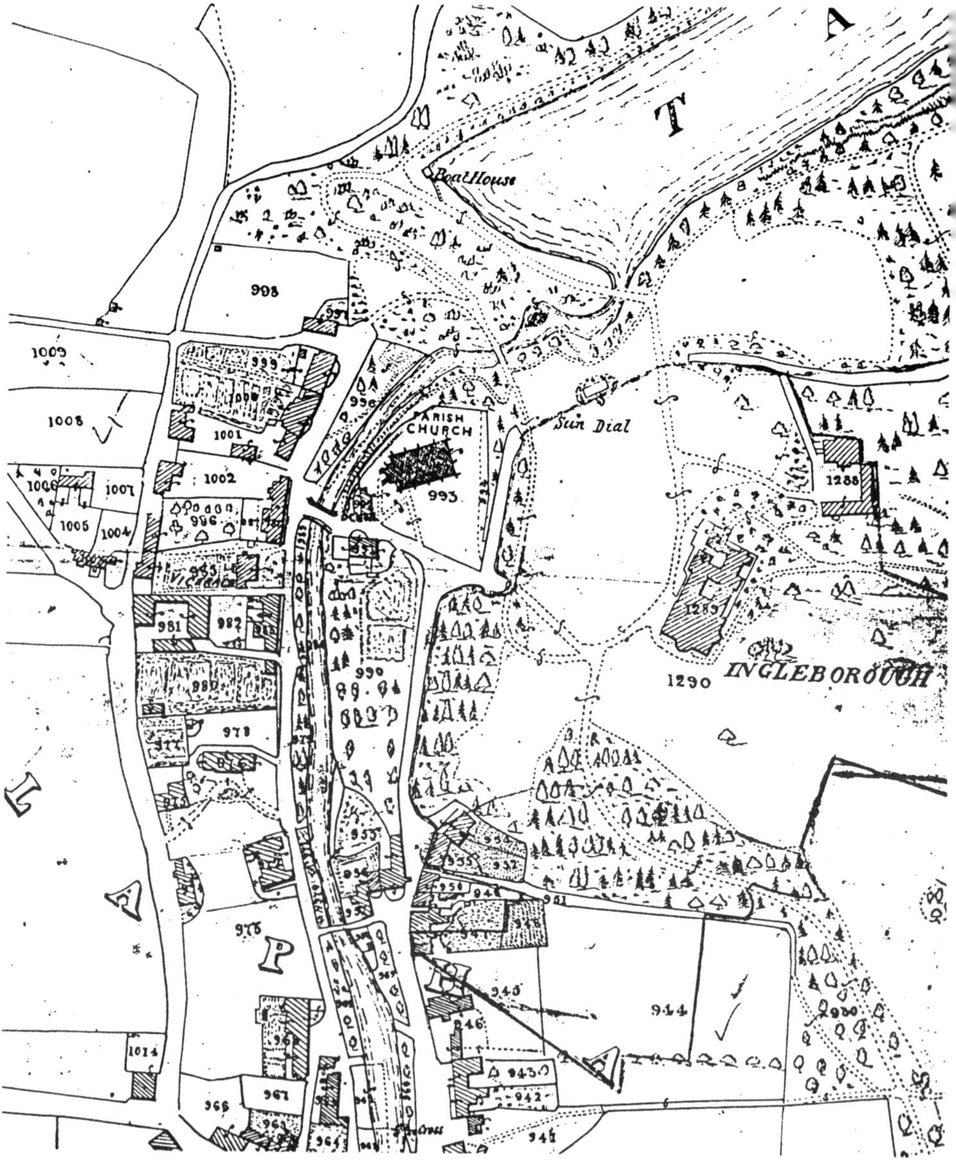

This page: Tithe Award, 1857, Ingleborough Estate Office. *Opposite page—above:* Ingleborough Hall when it was the home of the Farrer family; *below:* St Leonard's, Chapel-le-Dale, in the yard of which about 200 interments took place of men, women and children who died locally during the construction of the Settle-Carlisle railway.

INGLEBOROUGH, CLAPHAM

Conquest of Gaping Gill. *Opposite page:* A Victorian artist's impression of the main chamber, with a figure representing E A Martel, the first to descend the shaft (1895). *This page—right and bottom right:* Martel; *bottom left:* Reginald Farrer, wearing eastern garb. He descended with the Yorkshire Ramblers by rope ladder.

In Coronation Year, 1937, farmers with horses and sleds conveyed old tyres for the Ingleborough bonfire, operating from Cod Bank, near Newby Cote. In this picture, Ingleborough is seen in the background.

Main picture: Reg Hainsworth, of Ingleton, supervising the transportation of tyres for the 1977 bonfire, several tractors and trailers having been mustered. Reg was one of the original four wardens of what became the Cave Rescue Organisation. *Inset:* Godfrey Wilson, another keen potholer of the 1930s who became a warden. The remaining two were Norman Thornber and Tot Lord, of Settle.

Farmers who lived in the Clapham and Newby area appointed Charlie Mason as shepherd. He visited Ingleborough daily until clipping time, when the number of visits was left to his discretion. He attended when farmers gathered their sheep for clipping, dipping, spaining [separating ewes from their lambs] and the collection of the draft animals [those to be sold to lowland farmers].

Traditionally, a farmer kept as many sheep on Ingleborough as he could winter on low ground near his farm. The presence of sheep at their winter grazings along the rim of the hill did not save hundreds of them from a lingering death in snow drifts when, in the early part of 1947, the worst blizzards in living memory heaped up snow into enormous drifts.

At that time, 'if you had a good dog that would set sheep, it was worth its weight in gold.' Sheep in their snow caves 'lost a terrible lot o' weight. It was lack of water that did 'em.' When the thaw came, and the sheep had access to food, they quickly rallied and the lambing time of 1947 was one of the best on record.

The travelling folk (gipsies or potters) who were in the district when the melting snow revealed hundreds of dead sheep saw a chance to make some money. They stripped wool from dead sheep, spreading the wool around their caravans to dry in the spring sunshine and breezes. You could almost cut the smell of those sheep. 'When one of them potters came to our farmhouse wi' his billy-can for hot water, so he could make a drink of tea, the sheep-smell was awful. I was glad when he went.'

Jim Smith, who farmed at Whinny Mire, on the edge of Newby Moor, recalls that the grim winter began with 'a wet back-end.' In February, the snow began to fall, the wind drifted it and the frost stung hard at night. Farmers along the edge of Ingleborough got their milk away on horse-drawn sleds, making gaps in walls so that they could take a route through the fields.

One farmer who was not too particular about looking about his sheep in winter devoted most of his energies to caring for horses. When a local farmer visited the farm, he saw dead sheep protruding from the melting drifts. The horses were eating the wool off the sheep bodies. Hungry rabbits made for the farm buildings, some entering the barns. 'Those rabbits were really hungered—all skin and bone.'

The number of farms has been whittled down through changing social and economic circumstances. The Ingleton farms include many with delightful names—Goat Gap, Sunderlands, High Lea, Holly Platt, Slatenber, Yarlsber, Brackenber and Nutgill. Some of them have been amalgamated.

An Ingleton farmer runs sheep on Lead Mine Moss, above Skirwith. 'It's all open; you can walk from one end to the other.' Sheep belonging to the farmer at Whinney Mire were 'on Crina Bottom rocks' and 'we bought a lot of land at Skirwith.' A special problem was recovering sheep which fell into potholes, such as Long Kin on Newby Moss. Jimmy Sutton, of Holly Platt, kept the ropes which Ingleton farmers had bought 'specially for t'job.'

Over in North Ribblesdale, farms such as South House, Borrins and Selside have their handy tracts of fell, with dividing walls to restrain any footloose sheep. The old Furness grange which became Ingman Lodge or Lodge Hall is still a large sheep farm. The hill rights were on Blea Moor.

In a Newby landowners' book of the seventeenth century is a note about boundary walking, including a mention of boundary stones. At Newby Moss, where large stones might vanish in the ooze, a line of oaken posts was driven into the ground. Newby boundary extends to a small cairn on Little Ingleborough and comes to a point on Ingleborough itself, where it is flanked by the parish of Ingleton. The boundary between Newby and Clapham descends to Know Gap Sike and the Sand Hole by the old Clapham-Ingleton road.

Know Gap, above Newby Cote, and 'in t'corner of t'fell', was once a little farm 'way before t'turn of t'century.' Only a barn survives—along with memories of the last farmer, a Mr Coates.

The grandfather of one of the present Newby farmers went by train from Clapham to Borwick, to visit some relatives at nearby Holme. He disembarked at Borwick and, before setting off on foot to the farm, he shouted up to the signalman in his box: 'What's t'next train time for Clapham?' The signalman was interested. In conversation, he said he had been born at Know Gap.

Gathering the Ingleborough sheep is a spectacular event, with the farmers of Ingleton, Newby and Clapham collaborating to bring down several thousand sheep, for dipping, spaining [taking away the lambs from the ewes], clipping, to draw off draft ewes for fattening before the Christmas sales or, in early November, for tupping. The Clapham farmers meet in March to set the gathering dates and the other men 'go in with them.' Three gathering points are used—Know Gap, Bleak Bank and Cod Bank at Cold Cotes.

The sheep come down 'without any bother', but if it's a hot day in June the men go up the fell at 3 a.m. so that they are back down at 6-30, 'before sun gets up.' Otherwise the sheep are inclined to hang about in the shade of rocks or in 'little nook holes'. And the dogs get jiggered as well.

No longer do the Newby men employ a shepherd; they do the work themselves on a rota system. When the sheep have gone out in the spring, at the end of May, they are shepherded every day to see the lambs are keeping up and the hoggs [last year's lambs] do not get rigged [lying helplessly on their backs] under the peat hags. 'The hoggs are full of wool and cannot right themselves again. We have to leuk t'ground every day till clipping time.'

If there is a dry spring, the farmer drives the sheep up on to the moss, where the water is available. 'We get lambs down potholes so we have to leuk them every day, almost, but we also have hikers who have seen or heard a lamb down a pothole calling to report it. So we get Cave Rescue Organisation out. . .'

Ingleborough Management Committee looks after Storrs Common and Cold Cotes Waste. The Waste, which the district council 'posted' off from the road to keep off caravanners, also provides access to various fields. Years ago, the horses of the travelling folk grazed the Waste 'down to t'wick'. Since posts have been driven into the road verge to prevent intrusion, heather has begun to return.

Jim Smith recalls when the Ingleborough walls were in poor shape and 'there'd be some sheep right across at Ribblehead. Then the walls were mended. I took men up to near Dale House [near Chapel-le-Dale Church] in a Land Rover. They hadn't far to walk on to the fell from here.'

Gathering to individual pens at Cold Cotes 'used to be a heck of a job. . .then we put a 'shedder' in and there was no work at all.' Every man stood at his own gate and diverted his stock into his own pen by nimbly moving the gate backwards and forwards. The sheep got to know their own pens.

Each flock of sheep has its own distinctive mark of ownership. For example, when Edward Dawson bought a farm in Cold Cotes in 1879, moving here and establishing his sheep-mark in 1884, each sheep had the letter D on the near rib and a red patch on the rump. The local sheep guide, a booklet detailing the marks of each flock, was revised a few years ago. Any number of small farms have been amalgamated to create much larger units.

Peat was the fuel which kept the grates of local farms warm. Digging out peat from a moss was 'a mucky job'. A turf barrow was used between the diggings and the dry ground where turves were set-up, one against another, to be dried off by wind or sun. The last time Newby Moss was gripped [drained, using an open cut] by hand was about the time of the 1914-18 war. Bill Grimshaw and Bill Marklew dealt with an acre or two, the water being directed into various potholes.

Washing sheep was carried out about a fortnight before clipping; it got rid of the particles of dirt picked up on the hill and also, in times long gone, the last traces of the salve, a mixture of tar and butter laboriously applied to the skin of sheep in November. The beck at Cold Cotes was dammed up. Another wash-dub lay near the main road at Newby.

The post-haytime work included mowing and transporting rushes from the common: these were for bedding down the young stock. A horse and sled were used and the farmer tied a scythe and rake to the sled. 'Anyone who got a sled load of light, springy rushes in a day thought he was doing well.'

Ted Dawson recalls: 'The farmer who finished haytime first got the chance of mowing the rushes nearest to the fell gate, not far from home. As time went on, mowing was taking place in Cote Gill or beyond.'

In the old days, there was much work for horses. A North Ribblesdale tradition holds that the Colt Park farm was so named because of an old association with young animals. In monastic times, when Furness Abbey had the land, what is now Lodge Hall was a grange, where horse-rearing took place. The young horses were taken to Colt Park, an enclosure.

Newby and Clapham farmers ran their horses on Ingleborough, for a few weeks after haytime. 'They would go and catch them when they wanted them for the back-end work. They didn't take much catching with a bit o' cake and a bucket. I should think they were ready for coming off.'

Mr Booth, of Nether Lodge, in North Ribblesdale, drove some stags [young horses] to Sulber for summer grazing. Mrs Betsy Mason, of Lodge Hall, recalls them passing the farm on their way to the flanks of Ingleborough. 'He used to have quite a few stags and he was always breaking them in.'

The drum-like hooves of a horse quickly poach [puddle] any damp ground. When Mrs Mason and her husband moved to Lodge Hall, 'we had to sign a contract and one of the clauses was that we hadn't to have horses in the meadows.'

Now a farmer climbs on to his all-terrain vehicle and, with his dog riding pillion, can reach virtually any part of the common without being out of breath.

Miners and Quarrymen

DAME ALICE KETYLL knew where all the lead and silver mines of Ingleborough Hill were to be found. Alice, who lived in the fifteenth century, was the Clapham witch and her stepson John de Clapham lived at Clapdale Castle. In the spring of 1468, she was persuaded by John to obtain for him five hundred horsemen, arms and money to assist him in the Lancastrian cause during the Wars of the Roses.

Clapdale.

After a short, bloody career at arms, John de Clapham was taken by the Yorkists and beheaded without trial. Clapdale Castle was put to the torch [or so the story goes] and Dame Alice found guilty of witchcraft. As a penalty, she revealed the whereabouts of the Ingleborough mines, the proceeds of which were used to pay for the restoration of Clapham Church.

The story must have gathered the moss of imaginative story-telling, for Ingleborough has not been outstanding for its minerals.

An association with galena is perpetuated by the name Lead Mine Moss, above White Scar Cave.

Frank Beresford, who was born and bred in the Dales, showed me a piece of 'Ingleborough lead'. I asked him where he had found it. He replied: 'In Swaledale. Any galena [lead ore] from the hill was taken by horse and cart to one of the Swaledale mills for smelting.' It was a folk memory which had come down from the dawn of the eighteenth century.

Some documentary evidence was found by L O Tyson, while researching Marrick Priory. He came across two indentures or leases connecting Ingleborough with Swaledale. In September, 1703, John Blackburne, of 'Fryerhead near Malham', took a lease of land around Ingleborough from Henry Bouche. The land ran from 'Scaleber Yeat in the west to little Ingleborrow in the east.' Included was a tenement called Easegill, belonging to Thomas Butterfield of Yarlsborrow, and also Ingleton Pasture.'

Blackburne not only had the right to 'digg, delve, trench, sink shafts, drive levells or opencasts' for the purpose of getting lead ore; he might also erect a smelt mill, though this was never done locally. Blackburne's obligation was to pay a royalty to Henry Bouche, this being a tenth dish or share of all Blue Ore raised and a fourteenth dish of all White Ore raised.'

The implication is that a virgin vein was being worked, the white ore being lead carbonate, which is invariably found at the top of the vein where the lead has oxidised. Blue ore occurs just under the white.

Once the mines were in production, Bouche had the opportunity—on payment of an eighth share of the costs—to become a partner.

On October 4, 1703, Peter Alcock of Burnsall in Wharfedale granted to John Wilkinson of Halifax and Ellin his wife a fourth share of the Royalty and Tithes of the Ingleborough lead mines for a term of 15 years. The sum involved was £5. The Wilkinsons sold this fourth share to Blackburne for £510 on the same day, a most profitable transaction.

In 1704, two men were set to work, at 10 shillings each, to locate lead in the prescribed area. When a vein was found, it was open-casted and the ore was dressed ready for transport (at a cost of £3.16s). A further 16s was expended for the packhorse transport from Lead Mine Moss to the Cupulo Smelt Mill near Marrick in Swaledale, in which enterprise Blackburne was a partner. Trials with the ore cost a further £1.16s, which was money ill-spent, the tests being unsuccessful.

When, not long afterwards, Henry Bouche died, the mining project ended. The name Lead Mine Moss is a reminder of a project which, according to a sorrowful Blackburne, 'proved good for nothing.'

Seams of coal were drift-mined in the Yoredales at various places in the Dales. Hard, brittle coal was taken from Whernside. In the Ingleton district, coal was being mined on a small scale before 1600, much of it being used to burn lime in field kilns, the lime being spread on the land to sweeten it. The Tomlinson family were miners for over 200 years and worked most of the outcrops. James Barker, a pit owner, transported his coal to the screens by pony-drawn tubs.

Maggie Pit, Jin Pit and Moorgarth Pit yielded passable coal. Dolands Main, Grove Pit and Wilson Wood Pit contributed to the supply. The last-named closed in 1887, after being active for nine years. The workings were flooded by a stream which outfaced the pumps.

The New Colliery transformed the Ingleton skyline. In 1913, two shafts were sunk to a depth of 300 yards, reaching seams which were 10 ft and 9 ft in depth. As the Colliery developed, the number of workers rose sharply until about 500 men were employed between 1917 and 1920. In one week, the output of coal was 2,000 tons. A ton of coal cost eighteen shillings and local people could fill a handcart for two shillings.

The Colliery had a fitful life until 1937, when it was closed down for good. Ingleton New Colliery had existed for less than 25 years and was defeated by the vagaries of the Craven Fault, which cut off the coal seams to the east. They lay in a geological 'saucer'. One morning, miners working the 10 ft seam suddenly came across white rock.

The manager told his men to blast it away in case there was coal beyond. When the smoke from the explosion had cleared, coal was found—but it was the nine feet seam taking a downward turn. Some machinery was removed, together with valuable timber, but orders were given for the pumps to stop. Miners descended in the cage one day to find the workings knee-deep in water. Thousands of pounds worth of machinery and equipment remained underground, but the shafts were sealed with girders and concrete.

Ingleton Colliery.

The slagheaps were planted with trees in a scheme devised by local Quakers. The New Village of a hundred redbrick houses, each house costing £91 to build, is now an attractive estate of mainly owner-occupiers. The houses were built in two circles with a grassy area at the centre.

The widow of a former manager gave me a map of No.1 pit. I loaned the map to a historian and it was never returned. Fortunately, I made a few notes. Five seams of coal are clearly marked in red. In a 'remarks' column were notes such as 'total water, 600 gallons per hour' at 113 feet and 'faulty ground' at 193 ft. The description of the strata provides another interesting column, the men who sank the shaft encountering 'strong white fireclay, dark clunch and shale, fireclay, ironstone and coal, dark shaley clunch and grey rock.'

More important than the coal industry to the economy of Ingleton was quarrying. At Meal Bank a quarry, opened in 1869 by Clark and Wilson, was notable for the method of dealing with the lime. A Hoffman continuous-burning kiln, of German design, was introduced.

The old Ingleton Granite Quarry in Chapel-le-Dale was opened in 1888 by John Scott and Company, being served by a mineral line, traces of which are seen by those using Storrs Common on their way to Crina Bottom and Ingleborough. For a mile to Easegill, a single track passed the reservoir and White Scar Cave, crossing the hill at Skirwith. A saddle-tank, *Northumbria,* was set to work hauling the wagons.

At Easegill, an inclined railway (gradient 1 in 6) descended to Ingleton, a mile away. Laden wagons, two at a time, had more than enough weight to lift two empty wagons to the top of the incline. On a Friday, in the comparatively languid days prior to the 1914-18 war, a wagon of coal was transported up the incline to Crina Bottom Lane, where local farmers with horses and carts collected the fuel. They had the week-end in which to remove the coal. Early on Monday morning, the movement of so-called granite—it was actually a mudstone—resumed.

The inclined railway was replaced by an aerial ropeway because runaway wagons were being frequently reported. In 1926, Albert Royston and his family were living at a watchman's residence in the granite quarry. The bungalow-type structure became known as the Black Hut.

Pieces of limestone from the pavements of Ingleborough have been lifted for use on walls. A Newby farmer recalls when farmers carted pieces 'for patching up the walls and buildings. . . Now that the pavements are protected, moving stone is illegal.' There remains, near Bleak Bank, a heap of pieces of limestone trimmed for use as topstones on walls. They were never moved from the hill.

Sam's Quarry, near Newby, was named after Sam Hellum, the last man to operate it. The quarry is now grassed-over. The Prestons of Ingleton removed thousands of tons of stone from the pavements of Ingleton and sold it to those who wished to have quality rock gardens.

PART 3

Tourists and Cavers

> A pistol discharged in Yordas Cave produces a report like the sound of a park of artillery.
>
> *Directory for the West Riding (1822).*

> The sides of the mountains in this part of the country are full of caverns, chasms and deep openings, of all sizes and shapes. Many of them are called pots, from being open at the top like saucepans, and most of them have their bottoms filled with water, from some stream that runs through the bowel of the mountain.
>
> *Priscilla Wakefield, early 19th century.*

A Trickle of Sightseers

WRITERS AND ARTISTS were the first publicists of the splendours in the Ingleton district.

A clergyman who signed himself 'Pastor' in the *Gentleman's Magazine* (March, 1761) became, unwittingly, the creator of the local tourist industry by penning an account which was the first to have a national circulation. To him, Ingleborough was 'a mountain, singularly eminent, whether you regard its height or the immense base upon which it stands.'

Pastor actually climbed the hill, though his example was not followed by Thomas Gray, who hurried through Craven after an extensive tour of the Lake District in 1769, having only time to notice that Ingleton is a pretty village 'situated very high, and yet in a valley at the foot of that huge monster of nature, Ingleborough . . .'

Thomas Pennant, antiquarian and naturalist, visiting the area four years later, looked at Ingleborough, 'had not the leisure to visit it, but was informed that it was well worth a traveller's attention on account of the immense caverns it abounds with, and the various plants very rare in other places.'

The artists included J M W Turner, who first set foot in Yorkshire in 1797, forming a close friendship with the Fawkes family of Farnley in Wharfedale. His painting of Weathercote includes the vivid rainbow which forms in the spray at the base of the waterfall on a summer mid-day. The engravings in William Westall's *Views of the Caves* (1818) captured the limestone grandeur as never before.

From about 1760 to 1820, those with money and leisuretime who might otherwise have undertaken the Grand Tour of the Continent discovered there was grand scenery in the wilder parts of Scotland, north-west England and Wales.

The clergyman who signed himself 'Pastor' in the *Gentleman's Magazine* of 1761 wrote of Ingleborough that the bottomland was fine, fruitful pasture, interposed with many acres of limestone rocks. 'As you ascend the mountain, the land is more barren, and under the surface is peat-moss, in many places two or three yards deep, which the country people cut up and dry for burning, instead of coal.'

Ingleborough was so steep 'it cannot be ascended without great difficulty, and in some places not at all.' Pastor's bravery was rewarded by a glimpse of the flat summit, which was found to be 'very level, but so dry and barren that it offers little grass, the rock being barely covered with earth . . . Several persons now living say that they have seen races upon it.'

Here were 'the dimensions of a house, and the remains of what the country people call a beacon, viz. a place erected with stones, three or four yards high, ascended with stone stairs; which served in old times, as old people tell us, to alarm the country, upon the approach of an enemy.' He implies that, in time of war, watchmen

were maintained on Ingleborough and adjacent mountains.

The Rev John Hutton's *A Tour of the Caves,* first published in 1780 as an appendix to Thomas West's Guide to Lakeland, was a noble forerunner of many often trashy guide books that followed. At a time when the literary air was clouded with romance, he looked around him with a mind which was capable of assessing scientific fact.

He guessed rightly at the marine origin of the limestone in which the caves and potholes were found, stating that it had once been 'in a soft pulpy state, approaching nearly to fluidity.' Hutton had noticed that the grey rock was made up of 'the shells and other parts of fish.' He, poor man, while wandering in high and lonely places, had to reconcile his geological findings with the standard Biblical account of the Flood, when Noah sailed the waves.

Hutton explored Douk Cave, using a ladder and candles. He then turned his attention to Ingleborough. 'Our distance from the bottom, where the steep ascent of this high mountain begins, was about a mile in a direct horizontal line over rocks and pits...Though we had many a weary and slippery step, we thought ourselves amply repaid when we got to the top, with the amusement we received in viewing the several extensive and diversified prospects, and in making our observations as botanists and natural historians...

'All the country betwixt us and the sea, to the extent of forty, fifty and sixty miles from the north-west, by the west to the south-west, lay stretched out beneath us, like a large map, with the roads, rivers, villages, towns, seats, hills and vales, capes and bays in succession.'

On the 'plain and horizontal' summit he encountered remains of the rampart wall, 'from which some ingenious antiquaries endeavour to prove that it has once been a Roman station, and place of great defence. Of late years it has never been frequented by any except shepherds, and the curious in prospects, and the neighbouring country people, who resort to horse races which were formerly annually held at its top.'

He noted the stones and fossils—'black and brown marbles, abounding with white sea shells, sparks of spar and flakes of entriochi; spars of various sorts, the stalactical and icicle in the caves, slates pale and brown and, near Ingleton, blue; black shiver, tripoli or rotten-stone, bloodstone and lead ore.' Ingleborough's sides ('where there is any') was chiefly peatmoss, 'which the country people get up and burn for fewel: the cover in general ling or heath.'

Continued on page 81.

Above: Mabel Sharpe, with potholing tackle, surveys a snowy Ingleborough from White Scar in the early 1930s. *Below:* A Buick car being used by Reg Hainsworth and friends to move tyres to the summit of Ingleborough. It was bogged down about a hundred feet from its destination and had to be rescued by a timber lorry.

An Ingleborough limestone pavement, with clints (blocks) and grykes in which grow many species of plants. Also rooted in grykes are a few trees, mainly ash and thorn.

Left: This weathered block of limestone in Colt Park Wood is known to some as The Frog Stone. *Below:* The lapwing nests on ill-drained land which the old Dales farmers knew as 'tewit grund'. In the picture is a cock bird, as evidenced by the length of the head crest.

Above: One of the Swaledale sheep which inhabit Ingleborough. *Below:* Sheep on the common at Ribblehead (Ribblehead station and Park Fell in the background). *Right—above:* Trow Gill, near Gaping Gill; *below:* Ingleborough in winter.

Opposite page: Frank Royston, of Ingleton, took this photograph of a rubber dinghy being sailed on the big lake in White Scar Cave. Some years before, a bath tub supported by oil drums was in operation. *This page—above:* a dummy representing Long, the discoverer of White Scar, in a constricted entrance passage which remains beside the tourist route. *Below:* Sid Perou and Lindsay Dodd filming in the cave system between Gaping Gill and Ingleborough Cave.

Walkers on the flexible boardwalk which prevents widespread erosion of High Lot on the popular route from Southerscales to the summit of Ingleborough. Walkers make better progress than they would have done while 'plodging' in peaty terrain.

The new folk heroes were the cave guides. William Wilson, of Ingleton, an old soldier, conducted John Houseman on the local tour in 1800. Wilson was 'a proper guide. . .furnished with the necessary apparatus of a lanthorn, long candlestick, &c., for the purpose.' He gave the history of each place which was visited. 'An account of his own adventure fills up the vacant intervals of time.'

Thomas Wilson, of Bentham, jotted down his impressions of the River Wenning in rhyme (1781), begining: 'The vale of Wenning I resolved to tread, And trace the radiant rambler to its head, Determin'd Ingleborough Mount to climb, And what I saw recite in homely rhyme.'

John Bigland (1812) soon regretted he had not employed a guide, and was 'bewildered amidst the rocks and morasses.' Ingleborough emitted water at every pore and 'is almost continually enveloped in mists, or washed with rains, which occasions an extraordinary degree of humidity.'

Some cave names found their way on to the land surveys, especially those connected with the Enclosure Awards. Early visitors heard of Long Churn, Jackdaw Hole, Hull Pot and Sell Gill. In 1847, 'Chapman's Hole' is recorded where the Midland Railway were to build Ribblehead viaduct. Could this have been Batty Wife's Hole, where the wee lassie used to do the family wash?

The real caving age began (1837) with the discovery and exploration of the farther reaches of Ingleborough Cave, near Clapham, by James Farrer, the local landowner. The Cave, now open to the public and illuminated by electricity, stands in the dry valley between Clapham Woods and Trow Gill.

Farrer, a keen archaeologist, had taken a practical interest in features as far apart as the prehistoric burial chambers of Orkney and the Roman villa at Chedworth in the Cotswolds. He had the support of members of his family—Matthew, Thomas Henry and a relative, John, the second Earl of Eldon, who was then Viscount Encombe.

A 'Cave Book' kept by the Farrers records that on September 16, 1837, torrential rain swelled the beck and created a flood at a record level, sweeping away sections of the carriageway and 'rushing out' of the hillsides in unexpected places. 'On the 22nd [wrote Farrer], took the men into the old cave to the extremity of it, which is called The Bay, and there broke a passage through the stalagmite that formed it. This opened to the new caves.' He had three labourers under Jo: Harrison.

Exploration went on speedily and soon the men had penetrated about 790 yards, two labourers proceeding to the deep water (later known as Lake Avernus) at 940 yards. 'Here James swam with a rope attached. The distances are given not entirely at random but by the length of balls of twine used as guides for returning.'

Robert Story of Gargrave gave poetic expression to his feelings about Ingleborough Cave, which he visited in 1840, mentioning in the course of a long piece:

A gem-studded ceiling
On columns of crystal appearing to lean,
Sides flashing with brilliants; the wide floor revealing
A pure water mirror that doubles the scene.

The Cave Book had some distinguished contributors. Adam Sedgwick, geologist, wrote: 'As a general rule, these caverns have perpendicular walls and often nearly flat roofs . . . The prevailing colours of cave walls are light grey or bluish grey, from which they change through every variety of shade into dark blue or bluish black . . . and they contain in great abundance coralling, encrinities, and the ordinary well-known fossils of the carboniferous limestone.'

Dr Buckland observed: 'In other parts where the water falls in drops from the roof, stalagmitic accumulations have been raised on its surface, some of which are very large and flat, resembling a cake of bees' wax, but more commonly they are of the size and shape of a cow's pap. In Ingleborough Cave, these stalagmitic accumulations have assumed various forms, some resembling mushrooms, some bottles, some pillars, some globes or balls.'

The exploration of Ingleborough Cave ushered in the scientific age. It was here that Farrer, Prof Phillips and Prof W Boyd Dawkins carried out the first experiments to determine the rate of growth of stalagmite, using the calcite feature called The Jockey Cap, which was still in the process of formation. Its circumference

Ingleborough Cave.

increased from 118 inches (1839) to 120 inches (1845) and 128 inches (1873). Boyd Dawkins found 'the most remarkable increase was that in height', the figures implying 'an annual deposit of not less than ·2946 inch. At this rate, the Jockey Cap will arrive at the roof in about 295 years'!

Walter White's book, *A Month in Yorkshire,* includes a delightful impression of Ingleborough Cave as it was in the 1850s. For a Berkshire man, White got a northern feel into his writing and some authentic 'Yorksher' into his quotations.

The fee for a single person visiting the Cave was half-a-crown; 'for a party of eight in turn a shilling each.' The guide was—yes, an old soldier, 'a good specimen of his class, civic and intelligent.' He collected candles from his home in Clapham and led the way up the lane to Clapdale Farm. Mr Farrer had closed the driveway to the public because picnickers had strewn the area with broken bottles and greasy paper.

White, holding up his candle, entered Ingleborough Cave, or 'what might have been taken for a glittering fairy palace.' On each side, sloping gently upwards until they met the roof, were 'great bulging masses of stalagmite of snowy whiteness. . . mound after mound glittering as with millions of diamonds.'

A strange illusion came over the visitor as he passed slowly across the undulating ranges which seemed for a moment 'to represent the great rounded snow fields that whiten the sides of the Alps.' The cave widened. 'We are in Pillar Hall; stalactites of all dimensions hang from the roof, singly and in groups. Thousands are mere nipples, or an inch or two in length; many are two or three feet; and the whole place echoes with the drip and tinkle of water.'

Stalagmites dotted the floor. Others, joining up with stalactites, created pillars. 'Some stalactites assume a spiral twist; and when this first occurs in the roof they take the form of draperies, curtains and wings—many shaped like those of angels.'

The guide struck one of the wings with a small mallet, creating 'a rich musical note'. Another had a 'deep sonorous boom of a cathedral bell, another rings sharp and shrill, and now a stalactite sheet answers when touched with a gamut of notes. Your imaginative powers stir whilst you listen to such strange music in the heart of a mountain.'

To William Dobson, making notes for his book *Rambles by the Ribble* (1864), this was 'the most wonderful cave in England. . .

A picnic party was at the gate of the cave, and a little flirting was going on as is customary on such occasions. In a while, the janitor of the cave appeared leading a party. . . each bearing a candle in a rude wooden candlestick. . . Those waiting outside were now admitted, each presented with a candle, and so we entered the dim region.'

It was with a quaint wooden candlestick, capable of taking three candles, that I had my introduction to Ingleborough Cave in the days of Arnold Brown, a small, pipe-smoking man who walked ahead carrying a storm-lantern. I remember the hiss of this lantern and the flickering light of the candles as they rested on such calcite forms as The Sword of Damocles.

The Farrer interest in caves did not begin and end with this 'most wonderful' system. Members of the family, also John Birkbeck of Anley and William Metcalfe of Weathercote House, explored other systems, the last two being associated with Gaping Gill and Alum Pot. Each man was able to draw on the labour and materials of a private estate to back up his subterranean excursions. Birkbeck, the most active of the men, was lowered 90 ft down the 160 ft shaft of Hunt Pot and several times descended Sell Gill Hole, on the flanks of Penyghent.

From the springtime of 1885, a major new attraction at Ingleton brought visitors by the thousand. With the provision of walkways, steps and bridges, the bosky recesses of the two glens which converge on Ingleton might now be explored with ease. The Midland Railway delivered hosts of excited glen-walkers, many of them travelling in special trains from Leeds, Bradford or Manchester.

In 1894, the year before the first descent of Gaping Gill's main shaft, which sparked off the potholing craze, the *Settle Chronicle* published an account of a descent of Alum Pot, near Selside, by Harold Dawson and William Townend, of Bradford, and Joseph Dean, mine host of the *Hill Inn,* Chapel-le-Dale. They used the approach through a cave system called Long Churn, which brought them to a point 100 ft from the surface, with a natural rock bridge to cross before the final descent.

Of special interest are details of the equipment they used. They had a wire rope ladder with a length of 42 ft, divided into three sections, using 'dog clasps' for safety. Being flexible, the sections were carried wound round the bodies of the potholers, the ladder being of such width it fitted immediately under the armpits and rested on the hips.

In addition, the potholers had 60 ft of knotted rope, 'also some short length of rope for binding.' The electric lamp of 10 candle power proved troublesome to carry because of its weight. 'There is nothing invented for cave exploring yet that can beat a good wax candle.'

Also carried were 'a liberal quantity of whisky to keep the cold out' and a fresh change of clothing, 'as we descended with only woollen shirts and knickerbockers.'

Conquest of Gaping Gill

GAPING GILL, the principal pothole on Ingleborough by reason of the size and majesty of its main chamber, has remained immune from fantasy, except for a strange, improbable tale published in a periodical called *The Lamp* (1892) of a man who fell down, miraculously survived and met another who had been living down there for two years, dining on fish caught in the underground water.

My first descent, by bosun's chair connected by cable to a winch, was at a meet organised by the Bradford Pothole Club. I recall the walk along a plank to the chair, being strapped in and then feeling the plank being drawn away, so that I was left dangling over the void.

Main Chamber, Gaping Gill.

The drum of the winch began to revolve. I had a sinking feeling, moving slowly, close to damp, mossy rock, and then quicker as the chamber opened out. Fell Beck had been diverted but I heard the hiss, like escaping steam, as the water dashed itself against the pebbles on the floor of a cavern which had the size and grand proportions of a cathedral, with the hole through which I had been lowered looking like a rent in the roof.

I stood on the floor of a chamber which is 500 ft long and 80 feet wide. Water tumbling hundreds of feet broke up into dark blobs and struck the ground like the grandfather of all rainstorms. A potholer went by, his headlamp giving him a resemblance to a glow-worm, except that the light was at the wrong end!

Sir John Hunt, leader of the successful British expedition to Everest, came here in 1958 as the guest of the Yorkshire Ramblers' Club. Standing on the floor of the chamber, which he reached by way of an alternative route through Bar Pot, he was impressed by what he saw. Afterwards he remarked: 'I was thrilled. It was difficult to appreciate its vastness. Gaping Gill was everything I had been told it was going to be.'

On my first trip into the G.G. system, I was led along the East passage to Mud Hole. Away from the main chamber, with the echoing voices of potholers and the hiss of water, all was silent and still. Occasionally my helmet slurred on the roof and I lowered my head, thankful for a timely warning of hard rock. My boots were soundproofed by mud.

Stalactites, like inverted candles, bedecked the roof and walls, glistening when the beam from my headlight fell upon them. As light swept the roof, a myriad diamonds were sparkling—beads of water clinging to the rock and contrasting with the thick mud on the ground. Stalagmites had grown upwards from the floor as lime-laden water had dripped on to them.

Calcite formations ranged from the crystal whiteness of those still being formed to ancient-looking yellowed stumps, stained by mud and peat and the hands of those who had passed this way. A ladder had been rigged for a descent into Mud Hole, which seemed half as large as the chamber I had left behind. A potholer fastened a lifeline round my waist and secured it with a bowline, the most popular knot in the underworld.

The worst aspect of descending G.G. proved to be waiting in

the queue for the return to the surface. But I had accomplished quickly and easily what John Birkbeck did not manage to do despite much will-power and effort. Birkbeck and William Metcalfe, of Weathercote House, Chapel-le-Dale, attempted a rope descent of G.G. about 1842. The men had the foresight to cut a 1,000 yard long trench [later known as the Birkbeck Trench] to divert Fell Beck from the shaft.

On the first descent, rock bit into the rope and frayed it. On a second attempt, Birkbeck reached a ledge 190 ft from daylight and became the first man to gaze into the main chamber, though once again the hempen ropes were frayed and an immediate return was prudent.

Gaping Gill was first descended in August, 1895, by Edward Alfred Martel, a small, bearded, zestful Frenchman. He descended at a first attempt in unpromising circumstances—an approaching storm. Martel, born in 1859, and a lawyer, began his speleology in 1888. He liked gadgets. Two years later, he was using a telephone underground. Scores of 'abysses' of France were twice as severe as G.G., which had been estimated by Prof T McKenny Hughes, a Victorian geologist, as rather more than 300 ft.

Martel used three rope ladders, each a hundred feet long. When, on the previous day, he found they were just 30 yards short of the desired length, he lowered the ladders into the shaft by means of a rope passed around two stakes driven into the ground near the lip of the pothole.

He descended with a lantern fastened on his arm, and with a package containing candles, magnesium ribbon and a flask of rum, sealed with watertight wax cloth and fastened to a wooden bar, on which the Frenchman sat. He also had a telephone and 600 yards of wire. He began his descent in the early afternoon of Thursday, August 1st., sitting astride a stout ash rod, to which was attached the safety line which was slowly played out as he descended.

Good progress was made until the explorer reached the Ledge, at a depth of 190 ft., where the remaining 140 ft of rope ladder lay in a heap. He had some difficulty in entangling it. Forty feet lower, and the vertical shaft ended. Martel swung in a wide and lofty cavern. The ladder extended to within a foot of the floor of the chamber, which he reached in 23 minutes.

Martel despaired of giving any idea of the view from the foot of the ladder. Writing subsequently in the *Journal* of the Alpine Club [May 1896] he recalled: 'There were no stalactites or sparkling diamonds of carbonate of lime to be seen (the cave is too frequently flooded with water for that) but an immense cathedral unsupported by a single pillar. . . One vast hall, 500 feet long, 80 to 100 feet high, 66 to 126 ft broad.'

After exploring the vast chamber, where he was impressed by the 'flashing droppings of water and the darting of the light through the funnel in the gigantic vault', he ascended in 28 minutes, to be applauded by a hundred-strong crowd, who dispersed shortly afterwards when the threatened storm burst. Fell Beck was soon in dramatic spate.

On his way from Ingleborough to London, where he was to address the Geographical Congress, Martel saw Harry Harrison, guide of Clapham Cave and gave him the story of the descent, which was forwarded to the newspapers. Martel noted in the visitors' book at the *New Inn,* Clapham (where he stayed with his wife from July 29 until August 2): 'On Thursday, 1st of August, I went down Gaper Gill hole, etc.'

When the centenary of Martel's descent occurs in 1995, I hope to be at Gaping Gill when potholers re-enact his ladder descent of the shaft.

Gentlemen Potholers

EDWARD CALVERT, of Burley-in-Wharfedale, a member of the Yorkshire Ramblers' Club, had intended to descend Gaping Gill early in 1894. Dates were fixed and postponed. He wrote, on reading of Martel's success: 'To have a ripe plum taken out of your mouth just when you are going to put your teeth into it is not a bit pleasant.'

Martel, a most affable man, hearing of Calvert's disappointment, said that had he known of the Englishman's plans he would have invited him to accompany him.

Calvert made his descent in May, 1896, signalling to his friends on the surface by firing a revolver. Then a telephone was lowered 'and afforded a much more perfect means of communication.' He and some friends descended from Jib Tunnel and improved on Martel's performance by exploring East Passage.

Martel's descent, and Calvert's spirited response, stimulated the Ramblers to 'bottom' every open shaft they could find. They also found pleasure in organising an annual meet at Gaping Gill. Photographs of them in camp beside Fell Beck, early this century, show men of resolution who did not intend to 'rough it'; they brought some of the home comforts with them to the flanks of the hill.

These gentlemen potholers—as I like to think of them—were in a Club which was primarily interested in rock-climbing. The veterans of Lakeland and Alpine peaks were soon 'mountaineering in reverse', descending the fluted shafts of Newby Moss and laying siege to Meregill.

Potholing was a pastime with such limited support that in late Victorian and Edwardian times, they might be the only potholers on the hill on their chosen dates. They wore tatty Norfolk jackets and tight breeches, to reduce drag. They donned trilby hats and wore on their feet heavily-nailed boots.

Bottrill, one of the Ramblers, invented the modern rope ladder. He watched someone climb using the old style ladder, with its hempen rope and twelve inch wide wooden rings, and he realised that a potholer never put two feet on the same rung at the same time. He devised a ladder of only half the standard width, which saved on materials and, more particularly, was lighter to operate.

The YRC ladders became renowned for their quality, the rungs being of turned ash, rounded at the edges, and the Manilla rope untwisted, whipped on either side of a rung.

Before the 1939-45 war, the Ramblers were still keeping to their gentlemanly Thursday-to-Tuesday week-ends. They could look back on half a century of impressive exploration. We can share their experiences because they prepared reports on their achievements for the Club *Journal,* which remains a model of quality, style and lucidity.

Meregill, overlooking Chapel-le-Dale, tested their mettle. The entrance rift is 50 ft deep and the system takes its name from the the pool or 'mere' which spans the foot of the rift. In 1907, Meregill Hole was challenged by the Ramblers but did not succumb to their repeated assaults until 1912, when it then became—for a time—Britain's deepest pothole (520 ft).

On Ingleborough, YRC members liaised with the Farrer family and virtually took over the hill for the duration of a Meet. Estate workmen, with horses and sleds, were hired to transport their tackle to the chosen pothole. A large quantity of food was taken. For special gatherings, before the 1914-18 war, it included half a sheep, half a pig and great big roast joints. For five days they ate like lords and did it cheaply, for no more than 17s.6d. a head. (With some ceremony, the left-over carcasses were thrown down the main shaft at the end of the Meet.)

Calvert, Grey, Green, Moore, Booth, Parsons, Rule and

Blackburn Holden—these were some of the Yorkshire Ramblers who pushed back the frontiers and gave potholing a gentlemanly aspect in the immediate post-Martel period. So many descents were made of Gaping Gill in this period that, in 1903, S W Cuttriss wondered if the main shaft would eventually be converted into a staircase 'and the half day tripper pay his shilling to gaze on the profound sight from the vantage point of the ledge, 190 ft below.)

In the summer of 1905, the winch was ignored and the Ramblers went down by rope ladder 'for the sport of the thing'. The following year saw four ladies in the exploratory party, the first lady arriving at the floor of the main chamber—upside down! Alexander Rule, writing in the *Journal* (1909), considered that 'an expedition of potholers to Gaping Gill is a matter of such frequent occurrence nowadays as to attract but slight attention from the outside world.'

Blackburn Holden, who died in 1946, had been associated with the Club since he arrived as a guest at the G.G. camp of 1909. He became so enthusiastic for caving that, as a textile manufacturer, he had cotton ladders made for him in his own mill and used them for an amazing solo descent—the only truly solo descent since Martel's venture. The elasticity of the cotton ladders was such that when he prepared to return he had to tread on umpteen rungs of the ladder before it was taut enough for him to proceed upwards.

For the annual Gaping Gill Meet, a marquee and bell tents were erected. Duckboards spanned the marshy areas. The toilet facilities were immaculate. For cooking, a member persuaded the Primus company to make a special stove with a three gallon container for paraffin. Dinner was served at six 'and, by god, you had to be there on time.'

The well-to-do Rambler might take with him to the underworld beef sandwiches, half a chicken, grouse or perhaps some smoked salmon, plus a bottle of wine packed in straw. A veteran of the 1914-18 war had an ex-Army water bottle with a horn top which he filled with—wine.

When Percy Robinson was in charge of catering, some twenty people had not only a range of cutlery but serviettes as well. The drinking water was brought not from Clapham (where the supply was filtered from Ingleborough Lake) but from Austwick, where good spring water was available.

The last of the gentleman potholers, E E Roberts, was always referred to as Roberts: never Ernest or Mister. He was a positive person, with a double-first in physics which provided him with a job in supply during the 1914-18 war. He was put in charge of boots.

Roberts became an active member of the YRC in 1908 and he used to say that in the potholing sense he was one of the second wave of explorers, following the generation which produced Calvert and Slingsby.

A climber first, and a world leader in opening up the Dolomites, Roberts brought climbing techniques to potholing. When he retired from his work in education in 1935, he still had some twenty years of active living left to him. Organising a Meet with the base at the Traddock, Austwick, Roberts and his men would do the potholes on Newby Moss—forty potholes, no less! He outpotholed people who were two decades younger than himself.

The Thirties Men

BY THE 1930s, potholing had become popular enough to have its own organisation and magazine, quite apart from Club journals. The man who brought order and an international outlook into the exploration of caves and potholes was Eli Simpson—known as Simmy—a Leeds man who moved to Austwick and subsequently into Cragdale at Settle, which became the headquarters of the British Speleological Association, of which he was Recorder.

When I last saw him, he was living at a house in Commercial Yard, surrounded by a hoard of records and papers. He was an obsessive collector. Borrowing some old scrapbooks, he stripped all the original photographs from their pages before returning them. Yet when I wished to borrow an engraving, he insisted on my bringing my photographic tackle to Commercial Yard. I did the copying work with the engraving resting on the pillion seat of my motor bike.

He did much notable work, including a survey of the Craven underground systems, visiting every known cave or pothole with his surveyor's tape and aneroid, working by the light of candles or electric lamps. Simmy also responded to the challenge of photographing the main chamber of Gaping Gill, setting up his camera on a tripod, then distributing about the chamber quantities of flashpowder. He opened the shutter of the camera and went around igniting the powder. He recalled to me that the main problem, in the ensuing dense smoke, was re-locating the camera.

In the 1930s, Cave Rescue was formalised. Much of the story has been published and need not be repeated. I counted the first wardens—Reg Hainsworth (still very much alive, at ninety), Godfrey Wilson, Tot Lord and Norman Thornber—as good friends.

Reg, who for years co-ordinated each rescue, came to the district from Bradford when his father, Joe, bought a cinema at

Bentham. In due course, Joe bought Moorgarth Hall at Ingleton, which he and his wife planned to run as a private hotel. Reg, being at a loose end, installed some petrol pumps by the main road and developed a busy garage.

He remembers when his father took him on his first caving expedition, to Upper Long Churn, and recalls 'the problem we had with the waterfall above Dr Bannister's Hand Basin. If you put your foot in the water, it splashes everywhere and drenches everyone down below, so you have to be very careful.'

Reg was a member, from 1923, of the newly-formed Gritstone Club, the brainchild of Cecil Wood of Bradford. He had met the local lads on Newby Moss.The Gritstone Club were doing Gaping Gill in the following week and he invited Reg and his friends to join them.

'The main shaft was laddered. The skill in using that ladder was in keeping it straight. If you kept your body straight, you were inclined to push the ladder away from you and made it hard work. If you held your knees outside, you could climb with the ladder almost vertically, as though it was an ordinary ladder.' The old hempen ladders with wooden rungs were 'great big heavy things, but grand to climb.'

In the early 1950s, Reg used his 8 mm Bolex camera in Long Churn and Alum Pot to make a film. It was entitled *Rescue* and the star was a dog called Sparky belonging to Joan Horsfall of Bentham. For successful filming underground, 50 volts were needed and this was achieved with accumulators—four of 12 volt and one of 6 volt—which were taken below ground in old ammunition boxes.

Once, having taken hours and much effort to set up the lighting, someone who was exploring Alum Pot used flash powder for still photography and smoked them out. The final scene being not as they wished, it was decided to 'shoot' it again, in a daylight hole, so the action switched to Hull Pot on Penyghent.

Frank Royston, who took some excellent flash photographs in White Scar Cave, recalls the quite different problem of lighting up the main chamber of Gaping Gill.

Norman Thornber compiled the potholer's 'bible'—a published list of every important system, with details of its location, dimensions and the tackle needed for exploration. Published by Dalesman as *Pennine Underground,* as the years went by it was revised, re-named, extended, then split into sections, each section forming a chunky handbook, and is still in print.

My special memory of Norman is in connection with the Cave Rescue Organisation, into which he drew me thirty and more years ago. My special contribution was to raise money to buy the first (second-hand) Land Rover. I wrote to the various newspapers who rang us up for information about potholing incidents. I suggested £50 per head as a reasonable contribution and, hey presto!—the money was raised.

PART 4

Six Ways Up Ingleborough

Clapham via Gaping Gill

WHEN, almost fifty years ago, I began work for *The Dalesman* at Clapham, I had a variety of lodgings, the first with Hetty Turner. Her house, which overlooked the Green, reeked of paraffin, which was used for heating, lighting and cooking. Clapham, an estate village, was in a time-warp. Scarcely any development had taken place for half a century.

It was Hetty who introduced me to local people, including two characterful farmers who knew Ingleborough well. Arthur Tennant, who had connections with Newby, was such a devout man he would never say 'Hello' because it was 'O Hell' the wrong way round. And in the Lord's Prayer he omitted to recite the words 'Lead us not into temptation' because he was quite sure that such a thought would never enter God's mind.

Ben Hudson's droll sayings provided the magazine with a fund of material. When Harry Scott asked him what the weather was going to do, Ben pondered for a five minutes, then replied: 'It could do owt'. When I saw Ben and his wife, in 'Sunday best', waiting for a bus, she said sweetly: 'We're going to Morecambe for a holiday, but we'll not be there ten minutes before Ben is asking the way to Lancaster auction mart.'

I switched lodgings from Hetty's to the House in the Woodyard, where Mr Shaw's work for the estate continued into the evening. For it was he who operated the switch which sent a surge of locally-generated electricity coursing through the public lighting system and also supplied one or two estate buildings. The amount of current being generated by the turbine, which was fed by water from Ingleborough Lake, was indicated by a needle on a large dial in the living room.

Clapham stands where a beck from the heights of Ingleborough breaks from the confines of Clapdale with a mighty leap. In times of spate, the water thundering over rocks near the church seemed to shake the village. Every schoolchild knew that t'watter came from Ingleborough. The hill presides over Clapham and protects it from the coldest winds.

Clapham looks old but the Farrer family, who acquired it in the eighteenth century transformed it in the early part of the nineteeth. They rebuilt the body of the church on a grand scale in 1814. The name *New Inn* relates to turnpike times in the eighteenth century. Before Clapham was by-passed, the main road negotiated two blind corners and a narrow hump-backed bridge, from which one might watch sea trout attempting [unsuccessfully] to leap a waterfall. One sunlit morning, my eyes followed the arrow-like flight of a kingfisher.

Clapham was served, as related, by the orange-painted *Pennine* buses. Rail travellers had to walk one and a-half miles from the station, where the Farrers built *The Flying Horse Shoe* [named after the family crest]. The organiser of a rail trip to Clapham in 1885 arranged for luncheon at the *Shoe* and horse-and-carriage transport to the village where, through the kindness of the Rev T M Farrer, the visitors walked 'through his beautiful grounds to the entrance to the cave, which runs into the bowels of the lower Ingleborough range for a distance of more than half a mile.'

Trees, banks and cavernous tunnels protected Ingleborough Hall, home of the Farrers, from the glances of casual visitors. What had been a farmstead was converted into a shooting lodge and then, between 1820 and 1830, into a neo-Classical mansion, with a domed apse jutting on to a terrace raised above acres of lawn and garden. Pillars and fireplaces within the hall were fashioned from Dent Marble, a greenish-grey limestone capable of taking a fine polish, the surface having well-defined white fossils.

Reginald Farrer, when a boy, had his interest in plants stimulated by his garden-loving mother, the former Elizabeth Reynell-Pack. She would feel a special responsibility towards a son whose physical disabilities, including a hair lip and cleft palate, made him a loner. Reginald's spirit is everywhere at Clapham. When he was only fourteen, he fashioned a rock garden, the stones of which were cleverly positioned so as to resemble a natural run of strata.

Later in his short life, and with George Redmond as his chief gardener, Farrer developed the Craven Nursery. Here were nurtured many of the species of plant he introduced to this country during his travels in the alpine areas of Europe and the East. He was a prolific writer. His passion for the exotic led him to own a succession of Siamese cats, to some of which he dedicated books.

He died in the wilds of Upper Burma on October 17, 1920. When he became ill, runners were sent for help. When the end came, there was only a Chinese cook in attendance. His mother, who lived at Ingleborough Hall until her death in 1937, erected a memorial: 'He died for love and duty in search of rare plants.'

The memories remain. When Winnie Guy, of Clapham, was a small girl [and she was ninety years old in January, 1994] she saw Farrer walking down the village wearing a broad-brimmed hat, a black cape and carrying a silver-handled walking stick, twirling it like a windmill. Rob Hird, another veteran, attended Clapham School and remembers going to a lecture given by Farrer, who wore eastern robes and spoke with a squeaky voice.

Several times, I have sat enthralled at Hall Garth, the home of John and Joan Farrer, as Reginald's lantern slides were projected for a small party of enthusiasts. And it was a joy to sit on the floor of the Hall Garth attic where much of the Farrer material was preserved and read letters he sent home from various parts of the world.

Farrer had an impulsive nature. Once, while gardening, he suddenly stood up in his old togs and then sauntered to Clapham station and caught a train for London. Here he contacted his family requesting that they forward him what he needed for an overseas expedition.

Winnie Guy's friend, Mrs Greenhow (daughter of George Redman, chief gardener at Ingleborough Hall in Farrer's time) recalled Reginald's mother as a small, rather dumpy person, something like Queen Victoria. She was kind to local families and, when two boys were ill, she paid for nurses to travel from London to Clapham. They were quartered at the *New Inn* and set to work nursing the young invalids.

I helped Jack Winton, gardener at Ingleborough Hall in the days of the West Riding County Council, to rid Farrer's old rock garden of its mare's-tails. It was a job which Jack did voluntarily on summer evenings. We tried not to notice that Reginald had ruined his rock garden by creating an island in the pond using concrete. Presumably, in his day, it was covered over. A redeeming feature was the survival on the island of a Japanese maple.

The approach to Ingleborough from Clapham passes through Farrer Country. A modest charge is made for entry to the woods. The path is shaded by trees and shrubs. Here are beeches, well over a century old, also oak, European box, holly oak from the Mediterranean, red oak from eastern North America, Spanish chestnut and Japanese maples, both red and yellow. Weymouth pine, western hemlock and European silver birch also give distinction to Clapham Woods.

Ingleborough Lake, created by damming between 1828 and 1832, was for 140 years the source of Clapham's water supply.

Reginald Farrer wrote about Ingleborough Lake being 'in a long winding gully of the hills that used to be one of the characteristic ghylls of this country, until one of my ancestors was lured by degrees, on the first pretence of making a few fish-pools, into so damming up the stream at the valley's exit as to make the whole glen one broad long lake. A noble work; and when the bills came in, he was filled with shame and terror and put them all in the fire. So that posterity has no notion of his lavishness.'

It was on the 60 ft cliffs beyond the lake that Farrer planted rare alpines. Some ledges were inaccessible under normal circumstances, so he used an iron ladder, which still exists. Where the ladder could not reach, he distributed seeds by firing them from a muzzle-loaded gun. Not many of Farrer's rareities can now be found in the old Cliff Garden. The Yew-forest is supreme.

A Settle man spread a rumour that a rose-coloured swan was in residence on Ingleborough Lake. Those who rushed up to see it found it was an ordinary white swan. The rumourmonger said: 'Well, there *are* white roses.'

On the limited amount of acid ground at the head of the lake—an outcrop of slatey Ordovician rock—Farrer planted rhododendrons and bamboos. The rhododendrons shout to be noticed in a flowering season from March to May. The bamboos may look incongruous to some, but Farrer pointed out that these plants 'are no strangers to the adornment of waterfalls in Japan.' Massed rhododendrons and groves of bamboos give the Clapdale gorge the flavour of a Himalayan valley.

A walker through the woods passes a Grotto, shaped as an apse, made from pieces of weathered Ingleborough limestone. The woodland ends abruptly at a gate and fence. Now the path lies between a slope with outcropping limestone and the beck, a feature of which is a dam with a ram pump which delivers water up to a range of buildings which originally had the name Clapdale Castle.

Dodsworth, a seventeenth century historian, referred to it as 'a great old castle joyning on Ingleborrow, which shooteth towards Clapham and was ye desmesne of ye Claphams in later times.' From them it passed to the Inglebys of Lawkland and the Morleys of Rylstone. It then became a farmhouse.

When Cyril Hammill was here, we used to discuss the old story of a secret passage. Cyril said the house, which stands on a fault line, has a small pothole to the rear. Perhaps the thirteenth century builder of Clapdale sited it where another pothole leads from the house towards the valley.

Ingleborough Cave, one of the oldest show caves in the land, appears as a huge gash at the base of a 100 ft high limestone cliff. The story of how the Farrers extended the cave by penetrating a stalagmitic barrier has already been mentioned.

In ancient times, Fell Beck, which tumbles into Gaping Gill and has a one and a-half mile subterranean course, emerged from the mouth of Ingleborough Cave. It then found a lower course and, as Clapham Beck, now emerges a short distance away from a low bedding cave. When a major flood occurs, water may back up, some of it flowing from the mouth of the show cave.

One of the most complex and fascinating stories of modern caving is how cave divers found the link between G.G. and the Ingleborough Cave system.

A human connection with local caves in Neolithic times was established when a cave known as Fox Holes was excavated eighty years ago. It seems that a group of people camped in this sheltered spot, for the finds included pottery, flints and burial remains. The excavators dug deeply into the glacial material on the floor, exposing what was once a large cave passage.

Perhaps Fox Holes was brought into being by a torrent of water at the time when the nearby limestone gorge of Trow Gill was created. This Gill, on the line of a major joint, bears witness in its width and depth to the power of meltwater flowing off the limestone plateau in the last phase of glaciation.

With the ground frozen, the water did not make a mark on the landscape until it had to descend into Clapdale. The resultant waterfall cut back into the hill—hence the formation of a gorge. With a moderating climate, the ice melted and the surface water resumed its old course underground, leaving Trow Gill dry.

Beyond the boulder slope at the head of Trow Gill, where the cliffs are close together, is a much shallower, grassy valley, originally formed by a heady rush of meltwater. The path leads to a stile. The eye ranges ahead to Ingleborough but first there is the sight of Fell Beck tumbling over a lip of limestone into Gaping Gill, Britain's largest cave. Potholers go to ground in the G.G. system using Bar Pot, Flood Entrance Pot or Disappointment Pot, which connect with the south-east passage.

Harry Speight, Victorian topographer, referred to the final ascent from Gaping Gill to the summit plateau of Ingleborough as 'a stiff and longish pull'.

Newby Cote via Harryhorse Stone

NEWBY was a grange of Furness Abbey and Newby Cote a daughter settlement of about the thirteenth century. The oldest recorded name was Caldecotes—a name said to refer to 'cold cheerless cottages', alluding to its exposed situation, with its back to the limestone scars and a view across to the gritstone and heather of Burnmoor.

The original primitive cottages were succeeded, in the seventeenth century, by stone structures, one of which has the date 1660 inscribed upon it. When I first knew Cold Cotes, Violet Farrer, widow of Sidney, the brother of Reginald Farrer, lived at the largest house. The Hon. Anne Farrer, last of the line to reside there, took the keenest interest in the Dales culture.

The walk up Ingleborough, via Newby Cote, is nowhere very steep until you scramble up the gritstone. Lower down, where limestone outcrops, curlews dip and call. The waymarks are old shooting butts and the path lies close to Grey Wife Sike, where water flows only after heavy rain.

In due course, a ruined shooting box comes into view. Such a building was made to a simple plan, with two rooms, one for the gentry and one for the all-so-rans. (I once came across a roofless shooting box where the class distinction was clearly indicated—the gentry section being carpeted with grass and the other with nettles!).

The line of butts continues. In due course, beyond the syke, is the Harryhorse Stone. I heard from a local farmer, W Dawson, an interesting theory about Harryhorse—that 'horse' is derived from 'hawes', meaning a pass in the hills, which this obviously is. At the head of the shallow valley there was once a settlement with several roundhouses and ancient walls.

Nearby are the dry shafts of Newby Moss. My old friend Norman Thornber, in his book *Pennine Underground,* named the shafts as follows: Fife Pot, Fluted Holes, the two Cellar Pots, Wee Pot, Pillar Holes, Rosebay Pot, Fern Pot, Cross Pot, Long Kin West, Star Pot, Bridge Pot, Trapdoor Pot, Cave Hole, Boggart's Roaring Holes, Thorn Pot, Gritstone Pot and Five Ways Pot.

Others have lumped three shafts—each with a depth of over 100 ft—together as Boggart's Roaring Holes, and thus they were called by the Balderstons, authors of *Ingleton: Bygone and Present,* which was published c1890. Why should such a romantic name have been devised? The Balderstons noted: 'On throwing stones downwards, these appeared to go much farther than the plummet line. At length there was a cessation of the clatter, but there began to creep upwards another dull sound, something between a roar and a growl in its intonation, appearing to come from a deep cavern to the south-west, hence the name...'

Ingleton via Crina Bottom

INGLETON'S era as a tourist centre opened in 1845 with the coming of the railway from Skipton. Joseph Carr, the pioneer publicist, is commemorated by a fountain at the roadside near Ingleton church.

An improvement society was formed about 1884. Among its members was Samuel Worthington, 'mine host' of the *Wheatsheaf.* His son, William, presided at the entrance to the glens walk when I first took the path to Thornton Force. The steep side of Ingleborough comes into splendid view at the intermediate stage between the two glens.

Storrs Common, which lies just off the Chapel-le-Dale road, at the edge of Ingleton, leads into the valley of Crina Bottom. The land mass to the north of the track is named White Scar, now famous for its show cave, a resurgence system with two long streamways feeding from sumps which are close to the sinkholes in Crina Bottom. The exploration of White Scar Cave was outstanding because this was done from the point of debouchure rather than from a hole high on the hill.

Tom Greenwood wrote up the astonishing story of how it was discovered and explored. In August, 1923, Christopher Francis Drake Long, of Cambridge University, was sitting with a geologist friend on Scales Moor, across Chapel-le-Dale, when he noticed some fissures and a small hole he had not seen before. A narrow cave was revealed. From it came a current of air, giving the young men hope they might find a way into the heart of Ingleborough.

Long, crawling by candlelight, almost immediately found the skeleton of a sheep. After 75 yards, a stalagmitic column was found blocking the way. Part of it had to be broken; the way continued to a pool, to negotiate which they had to slither on their backs, with their noses protruding from the water.

The candles were re-lit and they moved on until the way was blocked by stalagmites, some being of the delicate straw variety, an indication that the cave had not been previously explored by man. A waterfall poured into a chamber adorned by stalagmites which were toned red, green and white. Reaching a richly decked gallery, the two men decided to return to the open air.

On the following day, they returned with enough food and candles to last them twenty-four hours. Having greased themselves to preserve some of their body heat when moving chest deep in water, they re-located what was to become known as Long's Gallery. He made a solo exploration of the roomy system with its glistening calcite formations and arrived at the edge of a subterranean lake.

On another occasion, Long swam in the cold water of the lake with candles fixed to his helmet. As the water level was rising, he returned at the best possible speed. By now there was swirling water, which washed him against sharp rocks. Long re-joined his companion.

When they arrived at the head of the first waterfall, their progress was impeded by floodwater. For two hours they occupied a ledge, against which the water lapped, until the level fell and they could leave the cave.

Tom Greenwood led many a party to what became known as Long Stop Lake, the return journey taking about two and a-half hours. He wrote in his brochure: 'Old clothes should be worn and a change brought, as there is a certain amount of not very deep water to get through . . .'

Frank Royston, a local plumber who was fascinated by White Scar Cave, took some excellent early photographs of the system, one of them featuring the rubber dinghy used to traverse the lake. Prior to this there was a raft consisting of a zinc bath, a wooden framework and oil drums for buoyancy, which was an advance on Tom Greenwood's original design of a plank box with flanking drums.

Much time and effort went into preserving the security of the cave and if anyone who looked like a potholer turned up at White Scar Cave, he was sent packing. In the days when Mabel Sharpe (nee Greenwood) presided over White Scar, I was always a welcome visitor.

The superstitious Mabel once asked me to 'let the new year in', which I did. Year after year, Mabel rang to ensure I would turn up at White Scar on New Year's Day. I was admitted to the cave by Mr Flynn. I had to enter the pay box as well as the underground system. And then I would repair to Mabel's bungalow home, adjacent to the cave, for sherry and mince pie.

The walker using the Crina Bottom route is in a valley through which flows a beck known as Hard Gill, which issues from a spring at 1,600 ft above sea level. After half a mile, the water sinks into a crack in the limestone.

In 1904, as already related, fluorescein was introduced into the stream to discover where the water flowed. Seventeen hours later, the answer was revealed. It had entered the White Scar system (at that time undiscovered), thence into Ingleton reservoir and down the hill into the village. When the taps were turned, a liquid resembling pea soup was released...

Jim Smith heard from his father about the time when Crina Bottom had meadows and a small resident herd of cattle. Grandfather, J W Smith, who had a job at Bleak Bank, walked over to Crina Bottom to feed the cows in winter. During the 1939-45 war, a lady 'from over Leeds way' lived at Crina Bottom. 'She had a pony and trap and goats for milk.' When she left, the goats were left behind. They were soon taken up by someone who sold them.

The path from Crina Bottom leads directly up the Yoredales to the summit of the hill.

From Chapel-le-Dale via Southerscales

AN ACCOUNT of the visit by a 'geological party' in 1856 gives us details of a multi-talented local guide.

This 'weazened-faced old man' wore 'a brown napless old hat, in at the crown, an old surtout [coat], very seedy and out at the elbows, a waistcoat minus many buttons, a pair of corduroy trousers a world too short, and huge lace-up boots armed with iron heels and terrible nails.'

His principal occupation was that of schoolmaster. He was also the parish clerk. Without his support, the church would undoubtedly have collapsed for he was keeper, bell-ringer and choirmaster.

The visitors looked at the majestic scars of Ingleborough and were undoubtedly shown inside the old kirk in its moss and timbered setting.

Not a great deal is known about an edifice which is now dedicated to St Leonard. Furness Abbey owned much of the land and may have had a grange and chapel here. It was known as Wisewell Chapel, after the old name for the valley, but by 1677 it had become 'Chappell ith Dale'. In 1856, the Chapel-le-Dale parson was housed at Middle Scales. Two years later, he had palatial accommodation in a new vicarage, within a bowshot of the church.

The guide conducted his 'geological party' to Hurtle Pot, 'a somewhat muddy hole just behind the church'. The guide said he had caught many a fine trout in the pool at the bottom. At

Weathercote Cave, which is roofless, each member of the party paid a shilling to the owner, who had kept a visitors' book but discontinued the practice when young men wrote 'such naughty things' in it.

Over in Kingsdale, the guide was making an excessive charge for a visit to Yordas Cave, to the detriment of its rival show caves—Weathercote and Clapham. There was also the irritant of having to book for Yordas the day before a visit. The owner of Yordas Cave had no option but to reduce the admission fee to 'two shillings per one person and one shilling each for any number up to five, and after that number ninepence each. A slight additional charge is made for lights.'

If the geologists had developed a thirst on that summer day in 1856, they would undoubtedly have assauged it at the *Hill Inn,* which has been re-named the *Old Hill Inn* with justification, for it was a hostelry early in the seventeeth century. Among the regular visitors in the days of the Kilburns was Lord Tweedsmuir, better known as the novelist John Buchan.

At the dawn of historical times, a Roman road from Bainbridge to Lancaster came down Chapel-le-Dale. Seventeen centuries later, the road had become the Lancaster-Richmond turnpike. Now it is prosaically known as the B.6255.

The 1870s were rowdy. Hundreds of workmen, plus their families, converged on Ribblehead for the building of the Settle-Carlisle railway. Materials were transported from Ingleton. The dale road was soon deeply rutted. Those who died at the dalehead shanties were borne to Chapel-le-Dale for burial.

It is related that one funeral party, feeling thirsty, left the coffin in the road while they refreshed themselves on ale.

The churchyard was extended to accommodate the 200 men, women and children who died during construction of the line. Also 'carried to rest' at St Leonard's were Tom and Isabella Kilburn of the *Hill Inn.* They died in a car accident in 1928.

My favourite view of Ingleborough is from Southerscales, near the *Old Hill Inn.* Thick beds of rock forming the Yoredale Series loom in shapely fashion, culminating with the astonishingly flat summit. Extensive limestone pavements are worthy of exploration except when wet, for worn limestone is very slippery.

Southerscales nature reserve, which is owned by the Royal Society for Nature Conservation and is leased to the Yorkshire Wildlife Trust, is reached by using a stile a short distance updale from the *Old Hill Inn.* The reserve has some of the finest limestone features—scars, potholes, pavements—with ferns and flowers in the shady grykes and floriferous grassland round about.

Among the plant species tucked away in cracks of the pavement are maidenhair spleenwort, dog's mercury, herb robert and hart's tongue fern. Common grasses are sheep's fescue and blue moor-grass, the latter having blueish-purple flower buds in spring. Among the flowers are birdsfoot trefoil, fairy flax, thyme and the spikes of early purple orchid.

The path to Ingleborough passes close to Braithwaite Wife Hole, a huge conical depression, with a circumference of 500 ft, said to be the largest shakehole in Yorkshire. The sides of this pre-glacial hole are smothered in boulder clay. The cave system below is the end of Sunset Hole.

This is now an acid area, with heath rush and purple moor-grass, a little heather (mainly ling), bilberry and cross-leaved heath. Over a stile lies the National Nature Reserve of High Lot (originally High Allotment), where progress is rapid on a strip of flexible boarding which, though a little unsightly, does confirm to the contours of the landscape and conserves the moorland on either side which would otherwise be trodden into a peaty mush by booted walkers.

High Lot is one of two areas on Ingleborough where English Nature, having attended to the boundary walls, is trying to restore the vegetation by reducing grazing levels for some years. This will allow any surviving heather and other dwarf shrubs to recover and regenerate.

The ridge is attained by a steep but short climb. The stony slope has been roughly stepped to encourage visitors to keep to a prescribed route.

North Ribblesdale via Park Fell

IN ALMOST any other setting, Park Fell would be an impressive hill. View it from Colt Park, from which it was named, and it seems to block out half the sky.

The Sedgwicks, who were farming here in 1927, heard of an impending total eclipse of the sun, with nearby Giggleswick on the line of totality. On the appointed day, they climbed up Park Fell, but could see nothing because of mist. Returning to the farm, they were in time to witness the spectacle.

Park Fell is, scenically, just a buttress for Ingleborough, which—stepped and flat-topped—stands with all the visual power of operatic scenery. **No right of way exists over Park Fell, but a footpath meanders at its northern rim, connecting the Chapel-le-Dale road with the one in North Ribblesdale.**

From the path, Ingleborough is viewed across a jumble of clints with wheezy old thorns and other trees growing from the grykes. The path continues to New Close, passing across a limestone shelf from which is a view of the marshy bowl of upper Ribblesdale and the 'basket of eggs' effect of the large drumlin field.

On the skyline is the long, lean ridge of Cam, across the end of which passed the Devil's Highway, a melodramatic name for the ancient track which the Romans improved.

Ribblehead, with its *Station Inn* and railway station, has much roadside parking for those exploring the area. The station, with a new platform for northbound trains, is a useful destination for walkers.

The Settle-Carlisle railway, built in the 1870s, extends for 72 miles and uses the north-south valleys of the Ribble and Eden, with some spectacular railway works—tunnels, viaducts and embankments—on the fell country in between.

Ribblehead had its resident stationmaster who made weather observations, sometimes releasing a balloon to assess the height of the cloud base. He sent regular coded messages for the benefit of the meteorologists, who had few regular sources of information from the high fell country. For many years, from the early 1930s, land beside the approach road to the station was use for the Ribblehead sheep sales.

Salt Lake, the incongruous Victorian terrace of railway servants' cottages standing just south of Ribblehead, is the handiest way to Colt Park. English Nature has a full-time warden for Ingleborough and he has a base in a small building at Colt Park.

The track passes through one end of Colt Park, a place-name first documented (as a hamlet associated with Furness Abbey) in the early part of the sixteenth century. Colt Park is an enchanting place (though potentially dangerous because of the depth of some grykes). Permission is needed to explore Colt Park Wood.

In the area, thought not in Colt Park Wood, grows the coral root orchid. In the mid-1980s, a twenty-four hour watch was maintained on this rare plant.

From the limestone pavements of Ingleborough have been recovered human bones from prehistory and also at least one skeleton of a farmer suffering from depression who left home one night and was not seen alive again. A year later, his remains were found; the farmer had crawled into a limestone cavity.

In winter, the bare ash trees rake the sky and, with the mossy stones and walls, gives a setting in which it would be appropriate to play some of the works of Grieg.

Selside, a hamlet with a Norse name, meaning 'the shieling by the willows', had a most curious residence, situated in an area of limestone pavement just out of sight of the road. This was a London bus, driven here for Sir Albert Braithwaite, who bought the Selside estate and held it until 1957.

The unusual caravan was extended several times and became a comfortable home. It was completely re-built in 1972, having two dormitories, kitchen, living room and store room. When the bus was hauled away, the wheels were still capable of turning. The premises are now used by outdoor enthusiasts from Leeds University.

In the 1940s, monthly services were held in Selside School, which was also the venue for dancing. T'owd Town Hall is a barn-like building used for social events. The men of the parish used to play nap [a card game] here. Across the front of the building is a sign from the old Midland signal box.

Alum Pot, a shaft in a wooded enclosure on a flank of Simon Fell, half a mile from Selside, is on private land. A small fee for entry to the land leading up to the pothole is payable at Selside Farm, which stands in the hamlet.

On a bright day, rays of sunlight penetrate the luxuriant foliage fringing the mouth of Alum Pot and a rainbow may appear in the shimmering vapour rising from the depths. The stream which flows beneath a fence at the south-western end of the enclosure spills over the brink of the pothole, being dissipated in spray long before it completes its descent of 160 ft. The waters converge at the foot of the shaft, eddy in a shallow pool and form a series of cascades which are lost to sight at the end of a gloomy cavern.

In extremely wet weather, Alum Pot seems to be on the boil, like a witch's cauldron. In a hard winter spell, cornices of snow rear themselves over the shaft, the waterfall is transformed into a series of icicles and the sides of the pothole have a transluscent coating of ice. It is not the time to venture close.

An early (abortive) attempt to dive the sump in Alum Pot was made by the Craven Pothole Club, one of whose members, a plumber, adapted an old oil drum as a diver's helmet. The air was to be delivered through a common-or-garden hosepipe.

He placed the contraption over his head and entered the pool while a friend using a car tyre pump provided life-giving air. The buoyancy of the oil drum prevented him from submerging. When a rucksack full of stones was fastened to the diver, air could not be pumped in and the drum filled with water. In the 1940s, a diver using more specialist equipment discovered a narrow underwater pitch of twenty feet or more at the end.

The most popular way down Alum Pot is by way of Long Churn as far as the Dollytubs Pitch. Birkbeck and Metcalfe, the pioneer potholers, were familiar with this route in 1847 but their attempts—though commendable—failed. Professor Boyd Dawkins was to be credited with the first successful descent.

Horton via Sulber Nick

FROM HORTON railway station, the walker follows a waymarked route across fields, with a view of Beecroft Quarry, with its turquoise pool. The quarry, originally developed by John Delaney, is named after Beecroft Farm.

The path continues into an area with limestone outcrops and goes on to Sulber Nick, which was created along a geological line of weakness, the path passing between a picturesque assembly of clints, with marshy areas where lapwings circle and wail.

At Sulber Gate, a dividing point of tracks, Ingleborough should be in clear view. The path continues across the limestone shelf towards the Yoredales. At a shooting box, the ascent begins in ernest, though with a well-made path to lead you across the breast of Simon Fell to the summit plateau of Ingleborough.

Ingleborough Today

> Paths in the area had been reduced to almost impassable quagmires, valuable grazing was being trampled underfoot, and the special flora. . .was being lost.
>
> *Three Peaks Project Report, 1986-92.*

INGLEBOROUGH, with about 120,000 visitors a year, is being 'loved to death'. In summer, the hill teems with people.

A 'stroll' in 1887 led two Giggleswick schoolmasters to each of the three summits in the group. G T Lowe, the first president of the Yorkshire Ramblers' Club, thought of forming a Three Peaks Club during a Whit Walk in 1892. Four ramblers setting out from Gearstones on a July morning in 1897 completed the circuit in ten and a-half hours.

In 1925, the Gritstone Club added Fountains Fell and Gragareth to their route, which they completed in eleven and three-quarter hours. In 1934, Len Howarth, a young quarryman, won the first annual Ingleborough Mountain Race, taking an hour and eight seconds, which is not a record today.

Even in the 1950s, it was possible to walk on grass tracks and not see another walker for hours. I am glad I was not on Ingleborough in 1951 when officers and men of HQ Company of the 12th Battalion the Parachute Regiment (TA) drove and largely man-handled a Land Rover to each of the summits in eleven and three-quarter hours.

When Ken Pounder and I completed the Three Peaks circuit in the 1950s, we did so at a leisurely pace, walking on faint grassy tracks and not seeing any other walkers all day.

Then Ingleborough was subjected to mass attacks. In April, 1954, I watched F Bagley win the first Three Peaks foot race in a time of 3 hours, 48 minutes. The Three Peaks cyclo-cross was stimulated by the achievement of a 14-year-old Skipton boy, Kevin Watson, who completed the course in 6 hours, 45 minutes.

The boots of thousands of walkers were churning up the paths of Ingleborough, Whernside and Penyghent. It was at this stage, in the mid-1980s, that something was done about reconciling the recreational pressures with the needs of agriculture and conservation. A Three Peaks Project was established by the Yorkshire Dales National Park, in conjunction with the Countryside Commission, English Nature and the Sports Council.

Most of the effort was put into providing new paths on the boggy land between the limestone and the gritstone summits of the peaks. Their sub-alpine character, and the freeze-thaw effect of winter weather, proved too much for some of the chemical compounds used to solidify the peat. Lightweight woven fabrics, stone pitching, flexboard and boardwalks gave to the Peaks' walker a precise path to follow. It also allowed the land round about to recover.

On June 7, 1993, the Prince of Wales officially opened 1,724 acres of the Ingleborough National Nature Reserve. The clouds parted for a time. The Prince commended English Nature and the Yorkshire Wildlife Trust for demonstrating the crucial link between conservation management and sustainable farming systems.

Peter Corkhill, the Site Manager, mentioned that the first nature reserve on Ingleborough was purchased in 1959 by the old Nature Conservancy and was called Colt Park Wood. This was followed, some fifteen years later, by a second reserve when Scar Close was leased from the Capstick family.

The reserve opened by the Prince of Wales combined these two original sites with land purchased in recent years at High Lot,

Southerscales, Park Fell, South House and grazing around Sulber—an area of some 2,000 acres.

The actual opening ceremony involved the removal of a flag from an engraved stone cairn. The cairn stands beside the path entering the area from near the *Hill Inn.* Those who continue through Southerscales to High Lot and the summit of Ingleborough become familiar with the clonk, clonk of booted feet against flexboard, which makes progress across the peaty ground quicker and conserves the landscape.

Boots have scraped the vegetation from the summit of the hill and have made a broad, dirty mark from Gaping Gill to Little Ingleborough. There is subterranean traffic. Cave-divers forged a link between G.G and Ingleborough Cave. The latest edition of *Northern Caves* comments‹ 'To date this is still a divers-only route, but persistence may yet provide a way through for lesser mortals.'

The Cave Rescue Organisation, founded in 1935, has since then been called out to incidents involving 2,163 people (aged from five months to 84 years), 150 lambs, 128 sheep, 47 dogs, 9 ducks, 9 calves, 7 cows, 1 bullock and 1 cat. When a 72-year-old walker collapsed at the bottom of the Swine Tail on Ingleborough, he was evacuated by a Sea King helicopter of 202 Squadron of the R.A.F.

Modern technology is readily adopted. The Molefone, developed at Lancaster University, will operate through 200m of solid rock.

Hill farming continues, with fewer, larger farms, smaller farming families, and a change from milking herds to sucklers [for beef production]. With artificial fertilisers most of the old 'flower fields' which gave Ingleborough an attractive foreground in summer have disappeared.

Hill sheep have developed an appetite for sandwiches and liquorice allsorts. The old heaf-going system is disturbed whenever someone brings strange sheep into the district. An increasing number of lambs are being taken by foxes.

When English Nature set up the Ingleborough Nature Reserve, it was decided not to farm the area directly, as in some other areas, but to attempt to design grazing programmes which would benefit the flora and at the same time make grazing available for the stock of local farmers To do this depends on boundaries being stock-proof. Peter Corkhill says' 'We have inherited responsibility for more than 26 miles of walls and fences.'

It's a mechanical age. Tractors wipe their feet in many places. Land Rovers bounce and bump their way to Gaping Gill. The ubiquitous all-terrain vehicle caters for the modern obsession with speed. Mountain bikes leave patterned ruts on paths where such bikes have no official right to go. The Ingleborough sheep do not even look up when a military aircraft on manoevres almost strokes the hill and rouses every echo in the district.

The main hope for Ingleborough is the work of English Nature which, in its efforts to conserve the most outstanding areas of limestone pavement, is complying with the traditional farming methods to re-create some of the flower-rich meadowland. This is being done by controlling grazing to the levels which formerly sustained a diverse wildlife and plants.

A traditional hay regime is now practised at a field at Colt Park after years of heavy grazing. Within two years, banks of globe flowers had appeared. Durham University is collaborating with English Nature over studying various grazing regimes and their effect on the sward.

I end my study of Ingleborough with some words used by an old friend, Frederic Riley, in one of his local booklets: 'So once again I left the hill whose familiar form keeps guard over the district which we love and, though as old as time itself, bears all the freshness of eternal youth.'

Acknowledgements...

Much help was received from Peter Corkill, of English Nature; Ted Dawson. W Dawson; John and Joan Farrer; Peter Fox; Reg and Alice Hainsworth; Clifford and Muriel Humphries; Alan King; Stan Lawrence; John Lovett; Colin Pomfret; Frank Royston; Bob Swallow.

Drawings by Peter Fox and Godfrey Wilson.
Map and diagrams by David Leather.